EMBROIDERY
EMBELLISHMENTS

by
Machine

EMBROIDERY EMBELLISHMENTS

by
Machine

Great Projects from Worldwide Designers

Viking Sewing Machines Inc. / Sewing Information Resources
Westlake, Ohio   St. Charles, IL

A HUSQVARNA VIKING / SIR KEEPING THE WORLD SEWING BOOK

Sewing Information Resources
President: JoAnn Pugh-Gannon

Viking Sewing Machines Inc.
Senior Vice President Sales and Marketing: Stan Ingraham
Publicity Director: Nancy Jewell

EMBROIDERY EMBELLISHMENTS BY MACHINE was produced in conjunction with:
Graphic Design: Ernie Shelton, Shelton Design Studios
Photography: Kaz Ayukawa, K Graphics
Additional sample-making: Pam Hastings, Karen Kunkel, Jean Knudsen, Mary Hargrave
Index: Mary Helen Schiltz

Library of Congress Cataloging-in-Publication

Printed in China

ISBN 1-886884-09-9

TABLE OF CONTENTS

HOW TO USE THIS BOOK

This book is designed to help you better understand the embroidery process and have fun making any one of the outstanding designer projects included here. We are grateful to each of the designers for taking the time to create these wonderful projects for your sewing enjoyment. What fun to have the opportunity to see how these designs were interpreted around the world!

Read the following pages carefully along with the instruction manual that comes with your own brand of machine. If you have an instructional video available, preview that also. The more you know about computerized embroidery, the more prepared you will be to tackle any project.

Each project is designed so you may substitute a similar design from your machine whatever the brand. Enjoy the chance to mix and match designs or even try new ones. Once you have tried your first machine embroidery project, you will be hooked!

Have fun and happy stitching!

USING COMPUTERIZED EMBROIDERY ON YOUR SEWING PROJECTS

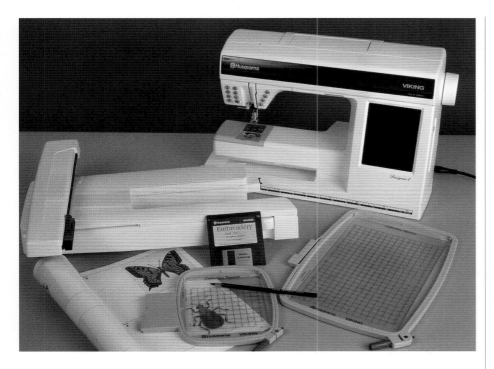

Understanding Today's Sewing / Embroidery Machines

Computer technology has revolutionized our lives as well as our sewing machines. Just as our kitchens are becoming more and more computerized, so too are our sewing machines. The tiny computer chip can control everything on the sewing machine from stitch selection with preprogrammed width and length, thread tension, the movement of the needle and presser foot, to indicating the thread capacity on the bobbin. It has made the use of our machines much easier while broadening the possibilities for sewing creativity.

The level of computerization, as on most products, generally depends on the sewing machine model and where it falls in the manufacturer's retail line. In the beginning, only the top-of-the-line sewing machines were available with any "touch-of-the-button" features. As technology has become more widespread, you will find different features of computerization on the less expensive models in the line. The ability to choose a stitch where the width and length are already selected for you is practically commonplace on most machines, as well as an almost limitless number of stitches from which to choose. A memory buttonhole has also traveled its way down the line of machine models. On most of today's machines, a computer screen is a common feature. A color touch screen, an automatic top and bottom thread cutter, or automatic needle stop up or down are some of the latest features available.

And when it comes to built-in embroidery, the possibilities become even more exciting. Over the years, it has almost appeared as if the more stitches your machine has built-in, the better it was considered. Well, today, the easier it is to produce and create beautiful, large embroideries, the more advanced your machine is. With the help of the PC (personal computer), your sewing machine becomes an entirely different machine with unlimited potential. Interchangeable computer disks, built-in customizing, digitizing, resizing capabilities, stitch editors, and 3-D imaging are just some of the software options for the committed sewer.

To begin simply, every sewing machine manufacturer produces a machine capable of stitching out professional-looking filled-in embroideries. Many machines will have a small selection built into the machine. But the true excitement comes with the option of using insertable disks available from each manufacturer as well as many other companies specializing only in embroidery designs. Designs can also be downloaded over the Internet onto your computer. The possibilities are endless. Format conversion programs are available making any company's design ready to use on your particular brand of machine. Your home computer has now become an accessory of your sewing machine!

Computer Software

Specialized computer software for each brand of machine is the norm and specific computer terms are widely used. Often packaged as an entire embroidery system, many programs are included together in one. Be sure to check with your sewing machine dealer to make sure your computer has a large enough memory, the correct operating system, and any other software requirements before investing in the sewing machine software. Often easy upgrades are all that are necessary.

By working on your computer first, you can *customize* your designs—manipulate, combine, rotate, mirror-image, and change the size of any design before you even start to sew. Move letters, change fonts, and change the text into different shapes. You can even work with a number of designs on your computer screen at one time.

With a *digitizing* program, make your own designs from scanned clip art or your own drawings. Another program allows you to scan photographs turning them into embroideries. Add different fill-in stitches for textural effects and beautiful results, or plot the area freehand for specialized stitching.

Stitch editors help you change your designs literally stitch by stitch. Individualize existing embroideries with pre-formatted stitch formations. And a disk manager transfers your designs to a card or floppy disk for use in your sewing machine. Print out thumbnail sketches of each saved design for your reference.

There are even programs that allow you to see your design in *3-D* on fabric backgrounds or garments, or allow you to scan in the actual fabric to be embroidered. By choosing different colored palettes, it is easy to decide your thread colors prior to sewing. Print out the design as a position template and sewing guide.

Resizing is another possibility with today's software. Easily increase or decrease the size of your designs to fit the area to be sewn. These new programs automatically change the stitch count filling the area with the same stitch density as the original design. But you have the ability to adjust the density or stitch length, or compensate for the design precision. Select the fill stitches you want for a personal touch. You even have the option of working in only outline format for more creativity.

An extensive *"Help"* prompt or tutorial is also there to answer any question you may have just like with most computer software. Many of these software programs will work with any brand embroidery machine but *format conversion* programs are also available to convert any design you choose.

Save all the embroideries onto a programmable embroidery card or, using the latest technology, a standard computer floppy disk for easy use in your sewing machine. Each design is now your very own, expressing your creativity.

Additional Hardware

Besides having access to a computer, a scanner is a tool that will help you in your embroidery designing. This additional piece of computer hardware makes it possible to copy almost anything—a drawing, piece of line art, photograph, or transparency, even a swatch of fabric into your computer. Use the specific software for your machine and transform this artwork into stitching (digitizing).

Many sewing machine companies offer small handheld scanners compatible only to their machines. These scanners hook up directly to the computer and the design shows up on the screen. Though limited in scanning size, these handheld scanners are a good and less-expensive introduction to designing your own embroideries.

The whole world is changing rapidly, and so too is the sewing world. The best advise for those who enjoy sewing is to look carefully at what you sew and what you would like to sew before investing in any new machines.

OK...BUT I DON'T OWN AN EMBROIDERY MACHINE

Before you get frustrated and think that you won't be able to make any of the great projects in this book without having to spend lots of money and buy a new sewing machine, a computer and lots of computer software, take a moment to read the following information. You can add beautiful embroideries to any garment, craft, or home-decorating item following this free-motion technique. You might want to try this technique anyway, even if you own a computerized embroidery machine!

There are a few different methods for creating free-motion embroidery, but we like this one best since it does eliminate any puckering on your foundation piece. We have provided you with a pattern and step-by-step instructions to follow. Read through the information first before you begin to make sure you have all your supplies on hand when you start. In fact, the supplies listed here are almost the same as for computerized machine embroidery.

Let's look at the supplies first.

The *stabilizer* is one of the most important parts in the success of your embroidery stitching. There are many stabilizers on the market and each performs in a different manner. Following this method, you stitch directly on the hooped stabilizer, which is then cut out and the embroidery is appliquéd to the project. Puckers are reduced and you will be happier with your finished project.

Select a lightweight, cut-away stabilizer for the free-motion embroidery. A cut-away stabilizer is better for this technique than a tear-away as you want a stable, long-lasting base that will withstand laundering and wear. Also, a lightweight cut-away will be softer than a firmer version of the cut-away especially when the embroidery is placed on a knit fabric.

Besides the lightweight stabilizer, you will also need a *hoop* while stitching. The hoop holds the stabilizer firm and prevents it from "flagging." Most experienced free-motion embroiderers prefer various size wooden hoops over spring-loaded hoops as the wooden hoops have a screw to tighten, adding more even tension on the fabric.

The *needles and thread* used for free-motion embroidery are the same as for computerized embroidery. The needle selection is broad and should be based on the type of thread you choose to sew with but a machine embroidery needle is the first choice. For most embroidery projects, 40 wt. rayon thread is most often used and available in a wide range of colors. A lighter-weight bobbin thread is used on the bobbin.

You will also need a selection of different colored *marking pens* for this technique. The different colors will be used to indicate the grainlines or directional stitching lines on the design as well as the individual colors of the design.

Sharp embroidery or appliqué scissors are important for trimming threads and the stabilizer away. A fine point and sharp edge are necessary for trimming close. An electric *wood-burning tool* or stencil cutter is an optional tool to use for cutting away the excess stabilizer. Follow the manufacturer's instructions when using this tool.

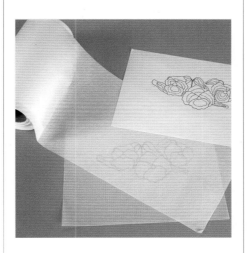

Let's get started.

Draw lines showing the separations in shades of color all over the design with different colored pens. Draw grainlines on the design using a third colored pen. (Grainlines indicate the direction the stitches should be placed while stitching each area of the design. The grainline should be placed parallel to the way the design "goes or grows." (e.g. A flower with several petals has a different grainline for each petal. If all of the petals were stitched in the same direction, it would not appear realistic.)

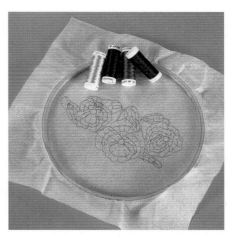

Loosen the screw on the hoop just enough to separate the inner and outer hoops. With the outer hoop on a flat surface, center the stabilizer with the traced design on top of the hoop, right side up. Push the inner hoop into the outer hoop with the heel of your hands. Tighten the screw so that the stabilizer is taut and free of wrinkles, using a screwdriver if necessary. Do not stretch the design pulling one side more than the other. Push the inner hoop out slightly beyond the outer hoop, tighting the stabilizer a little more, helping the hoop glide on the bed of the machine better.

Set your machine for free-motion embroidery by lowering or covering your feed dogs (consult your sewing machine manual for information). Make sure the feed dogs area is clean and replace the all-purpose foot with the free-motion or darning foot. Adjust the presser foot pressure to the darning position if necessary. Always start with a new needle and thread your machine as described before. Loosen the top thread tension so that the bobbin thread pulls the needle thread to the wrong side. On a practice free-motion satin stitch, the top thread should be visible on both sides of the bobbin thread, creating a satin stitch that is about $\frac{1}{3}$ bobbin thread and $\frac{2}{3}$ top thread.

General rules for free-motion embroidery

- Remember that YOU are the stitch length since the feed dogs are lowered and the darning foot is on the machine. If YOU do not move the hoop, it will not move. Although the stitch width can be adjusted as needed, the stitch length set on the machine plays no role in free-motion embroidery.

- A satin stitch is achieved when the hoop is moved forward or backward in a straight line. To achieve a satin stitch so that the fabric does not show between the stitches, the movement of the hoop is slow compared to the speed of the machine.

- A zig zag fill-in stitch is achieved by moving the hoop side to side, parallel to the swing of the needle. Most of the stitching used in free-motion embroidery is the side-to-side, fill-in stitch. The hoop can be moved faster than when doing a satin stitch.

- Always stitch with the presser foot in the down position as this engages the upper thread tension. When changing thread colors, raise the presser foot and rethread the machine so the thread lies between the tension discs.

- Use only machine embroidery thread since this thread is finer than regular sewing thread. The stitches will mesh and blend together better for a smoother fill-in.

- If both sides of the finished project will be visible, use the same thread on the bobbin as is in the needle. Otherwise, use a lighter weight bobbin thread.

- The design is always stitched background to foreground. (e.g. In a design where there is one leaf behind a flower and another leaf in front of the flower, the sequence of stitching will be: 1) the leaf behind the flower; 2) the flower; and 3) the leaf in front of the flower.) If necessary, break the design down further when there are petals in front of or on top of other petals within the flower.

• A stabilizer is used to prevent puckering and to keep the stitches and fabric flat when the embroidery is completed. If you are embroidering directly onto the fabric, a tear-away stabilizer is placed under the hooped fabric. A water-soluble stabilizer can be placed on top of the design when embroidering on a napped fabric such as terry cloth or velveteen.

• The width of the stitch is determined by the size of the area to be filled in. A small area requires a narrow stitch width while a larger area can be stitched with a wider zig zag. The widest zig zag should be 4 mm. It is generally easier to control a narrow rather than a wide width.

• The size of the hoop is determined by the size of the design. Try to fit the design within the hoop, but that is not always possible. The fabric may need to be re-hooped for larger designs. The smaller the hoop, the easier it is to control, especially when first beginning free-motion work.

• For each area to be stitched, position the hoop so that the drawn grainlines are parallel to the swing of the needle. Each area has its own grainline. One design may, in fact, have several grainlines. To make it easier to follow grainlines, separate the whole into as many parts as necessary.

• Run the machine at a moderately fast, STEADY speed. On many machines, the motor speed can be adjusted to a medium speed so that the foot control can be depressed all the way, maintaining a slower, steady speed. Most of the time, if needles are broken while doing free-motion embroidery, the hoop is being moved too fast for the speed of the machine.

• Outlining an area to be stitched first helps to stay within the lines of the design. After the outline is complete, blend the remaining fill-in with a jagged line into the outline.

• Blend the stitches and different thread colors by sewing a jagged edge over each "row" of stitching, creating the look of a "long and short" stitch used in crewel embroidery.

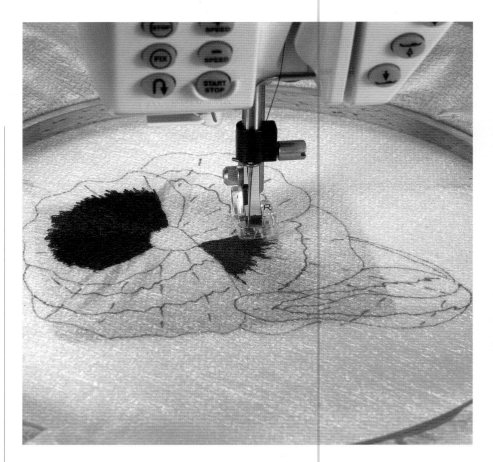

Your posture is important while stitching. You need to sit comfortably with the machine needle aligned directly in front of you. Sit so that your back is against the chair back and then bend from the hips toward the machine. Do not bend from or round the shoulders. This will help keep your shoulders from becoming tired and aching.

Place your elbows or forearms on the sewing table. If you sew with your machine on a table instead of in a cabinet, push the machine away from the edge of the table so you have room to rest your arms. Place your fingers on the hoop. Keeping the fingers ON the hoop is safer and allows for easier and more controlled movement of the hoop. The wrists should be up slightly, not putting a great amount of pressure on the hoop. The darning or embroidery foot will hold the fabric down where needed, avoiding skipped stitches.

Let's begin stitching.

Place the hooped stabilizer under the needle. Take one complete stitch while holding onto the top thread. Tug on the top thread pulling the bobbin thread up to the right side. Place both threads under the fingers of one hand moving the fabric slightly while taking several tiny stitches. This will help make a knot and make it neater on the wrong side. Trim the thread tails close to the fabric.

Position the hoop so the grainline is parallel to the swing of the needle. Adjust the stitch width as needed. Outline the area, keeping the grainline parallel and gliding the hoop with your hands. Run the machine at a moderately fast, steady speed and move the hoop back and forth to fill in the area.

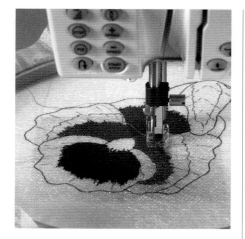

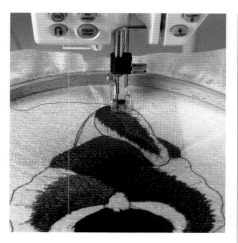

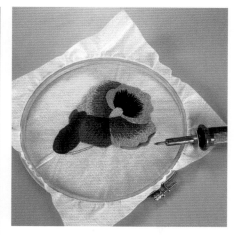

When one area is filled in completely, pivot the hoop for the next area, realigning the grainline. Using the needle-down feature will prevent the hoop from slipping.

Fill in each area, always stitching from the background to the foreground. To tie-off when the design is completed, change to a straight stitch and take several stitches in a row, stitching with the grainline of the previous stitching. Move the hoop instead of taking the stitches in the same spot since the thread knot will stay in better. A drop of seam sealant to the threads on the wrong side will help also.

Stems and very small areas that are separate from the main design are usually stitched after the design is stitched to the project.

When using an electric wood-burning tool or stencil cutter to "cut" out the completed design, stitch all the way to the edge of the design, covering all outside lines. If you are cutting out the design with scissors, leave $\frac{1}{16}$" to $\frac{1}{8}$" unstitched along the outer edge of the design. The stitching will be completed when attaching the design to the project.

Before using the wood-burning tool, read the manufacturer's directions carefully to avoid any damage or harm to you or your surroundings. Hold the finished hooped design in one hand and quickly trace along the edge of the stitched design with the heated wood-burning tool. The stabilizer has a much lower melting point than the thread, so the design will be "cut" out. Move the tool around the design quickly to prevent burning the thread.

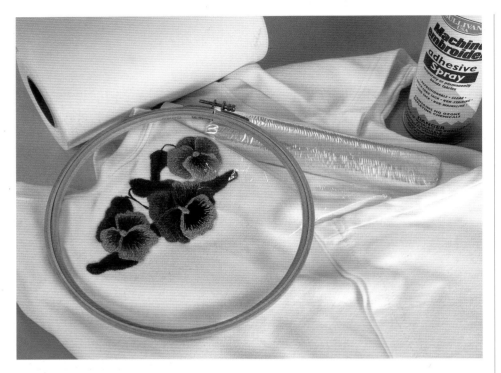

Let's finish our project.

If not using an electric wood-burning tool, remove the stitched design from the hoop and press a fusible web to the wrong side. Cut out the design along the design lines (remember that the stitching does not go all the way to the edge). Position the design right side up on the project. Fuse the design to the project, following the manufacturer's directions. Use a press cloth when fusing from the right side. When fusing from the wrong side, place the design on top of a thick padded surface. This will give the design on top of the fabric more dimension.

If a wood-burning tool was used, mark the correct position for the design on your garment. Spray the wrong side of the completed embroidery with machine embroidery adhesive and position at the marks.

If you are placing the embroidered design on a knit fabric, stabilize the back of the fabric with a lightweight cut-away and place a water-soluble stabilizer on top. The knit should be in its original relaxed state, sandwiched between the stabilizers before placing it in a hoop. An embroidery adhesive can be used to adhere the stabilizers to the fabric before hooping. The stabilizers will prevent the knit from stretching while hooping. Add a layer of tear-away stabilizer under the hoop before stitching. All of the outer edges should be stitched to the base fabric. Stitch, matching the thread colors and grains for each area. A straight stitch or zig zag stitch can be used for this step. Some stitching can be done in the center of the design to keep the design from pulling away. While still in the hoop, carefully tear away any stabilizer from the wrong side. Trim the lightweight cut-away close to the stitching. Remove the fabric from the hoop and carefully remove any water-soluble stabilizer. Rinse and wash to remove the remaining stabilizer. If necessary, lay on a thick towel, right side down, and press.

SELECTING THE CORRECT SUPPLIES

Needles and Threads

Needles come in a variety of shapes and sizes so choosing the correct one for your embroidery project is important. Most often, the needle type and size is selected according to the fabric you are working with; for instance, use a universal needle for most light to medium weight wovens or knits, or a ballpoint or stretch, for light to heavy weight knits. However, special embroidery needles have been developed for embroidery work and may be your first choice whatever the fabric type. Also, a Metallica needle has been designed to work with the new metallic threads.

The correct size needle is as important as the type. The thread must be able to lie easily in the groove on the front of the needle for correct stitch formation. Therefore, select the smallest size needle compatible to the thread

you are using. Generally, for a 40 wt. rayon thread, a #75/11, an #80/12, or a #90/14 will work well. For heavier threads, use a larger size needle. Always test your needle type and size on the fabric you are embroidering first.

Your thread choices are also varied. Most beginners are safe using a *40 wt. rayon thread*. This thread has the most extensive color range including a variegated selection from most manufacturers. It is the correct weight for most preprogrammed embroideries.

A *30 wt. rayon* is a slightly heavier thread, best used when filling an area on heavy-weight or darker-color fabrics, on enlarged designs that have a sparser fill, or for more dimension. As with the 40 wt. rayon, it is available in more than 100 colors, is colorfast and washable, and has a built-in "shine."

Cotton 50 wt. embroidery thread can also be used for embroidery. It does not have the sheen of rayon but may be the appropriate choice for fine cotton batiste, linen, or silk where a more subtle effect is desired. A *50 wt. silk thread* is also available in a wide range of colors for embroidery use.

Many of the *metallic threads* are a polyester-core thread wrapped with a metallic foil. These threads are washable and very strong, and come in a variety of colors. To avoid fraying at the needle eye, use a metallic needle in a size #90/14 for best results. Some other tips for sewing with metallic threads include reducing your sewing speed and using a soft, pliable stabilizer. Thread breakage often comes from the needle eye passing back and forth through the fabric and stabilizer, or a too short stitch length in the design.

Another type of metallic thread is a flat polyester filament metalicized to make it shine. This thread is machine washable but should be pressed using a press cloth at a low heat setting. The #90/14 metallic needle is best suited for this thread.

There are many other fiber combinations and brands of novelty thread on the market. Some are rayon and metallic twisted together, polyester neon, 100% acrylic, hologram-effect, and a fine wool/acrylic combination suitable for machine embroidery. These threads offer a different attitude to your embroidery from the straight forwardness of rayon.

The typical bobbin thread used is a lightweight nylon or polyester thread specially designed for bobbin use. If your design is reversible, a color-matched 40 wt. rayon works well in the bobbin.

Again, once you have chosen your thread, test it along with the fabric, needle type and size to make sure everything is compatible.

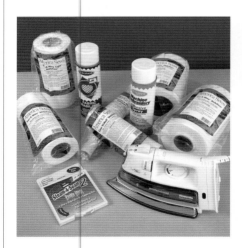

Stabilizers

There are many types and brands of stabilizers. After working with a few, you no doubt will prefer certain brands over

others but each type of stabilizer does have its place in the embroidery world. Stabilizers are divided into two groups—those used on top and those used under the fabric, though some types of stabilizers may be used in both ways. Think of the stabilizer as a means of strengthening the fabric while a great amount of thread is applied to its surface. In some cases, more than one type of stabilizer may be needed to "strengthen" the fabric and prevent any puckering of the design. Stabilizers may be woven or non-woven depending on the type.

Let's start on the top.

Water-soluble stabilizers are a thin film resembling the commercial plastic wrap used for food. Available in two weights, this stabilizer is used on top of the fabric to prevent the stitches from sinking in or distorting. It is often used on toweling or napped fabrics to preserve the integrity of the embroidery. Layers can be fused together with a hot, dry iron under a press cloth producing a heavier weight stabilizer. Once the stitching is complete, the stabilizer is torn away and then rinsed to remove any residue. Even if the fabric is not washable, this stabilizer will tear away easily. Often, a water-soluble "sandwich" is made with tulle or organza in the middle for creating needlelace motifs.

Heat-removable stabilizers are woven products that disintegrate with the high heat of a dry iron or press. Turning to a brown ash, the stabilizer is then brushed away. This stabilizer is used in many of the same situations as the water-soluble type but where a firmer foundation is required, when water removal is not an option, or on napped or dry-cleanable fabrics. When working with a heat-away product, avoid any exposure to liquid, as it will cause the chemical in the product to react with the thread and the fabric. A chalk marking pencil is recommended for any markings.

So what's on the back?

There are more stabilizer types used as backing than those listed for the top. The first, and possibly the most well-known, is the *tear-away stabilizer*. Available in a variety of weights, this stabilizer is used when the fabric is relatively stable and the action of tearing away the backing will not distort the embroidery or the base fabric. It tears in both directions for easy use and can be layered for more stability. You may still need to use a softer cut-away variety in the hoop with a piece of the stiffer tear-away under the hoop. A tear-away stabilizer is commonly used for appliqué, monogramming, decorative stitching, and buttonholes besides embroidery.

Cut-away stabilizers are just that—they need to be cut away. This stabilizer does not disintegrate like a heat-away or a water-soluble stabilizer, nor does it pull out like a tear-away. It remains with the garment through numerous wearings and launderings. It, too, is available in different weights depending on the fabric being embroidered. Particularly effective on knits, this stabilizer provides continuous support to the sewn design. Always test on a sample fabric to be sure you have layered enough of the stabilizer underneath. Cut-away stabilizers should also be used with designs having a large stitch count.

Another type of stabilizer is the *iron-on variety*. This stabilizer is used on stretchy knits such as sweater knits and sweatshirts. Because it is temporarily fused to the back of the fabric, any sliding or shifting is eliminated during stitching. Always check the temperature of your iron before adhering this stabilizer to your fabric. You should be able to easily remove it after stitching if adhered properly. Avoid using any air- or water-soluble marking pens with this stabilizer as the heat may cause the marks to become permanent.

Another type of iron-on stabilizer is *light-weight iron-on interfacing*. When a permanent, lightweight stabilizing effect is needed on the fabric prior to stitching the embroidery, use a fusible interfacing. Available in both woven and knit form, this interfacing is then used with another type of stabilizer before the final embroidery stitching.

Adhesive backings work best when the item to be embroidered is too small to hoop, too awkward to hoop, or hooping marks will be left on the fabric. The fabric is adhered to the sticky side of the stabilizer and another stabilizer is used under the sticky paper backing. Be sure to remove the adhesive backing immediately after stitching.

Spray adhesives are another means of backing your fabric with a stabilizer. Not actually considered a stabilizer, these sprays make the stabilizer adhere to the fabric without any slippage while stitching. Also use the spray to stick more than one layer of stabilizer together.

With the introduction of the embroidery machine, new stabilizers are constantly being introduced or old ones improved. Always remember—test first. Choose your needle, along with the thread, fabric, and stabilizer before beginning your embroidery project to avoid any disasters!

OTHER IMPORTANT THINGS TO KNOW

Marking

Marking your fabric for placement and drawing out the design require two different types of marking tools. You will find once you become more familiar with your embroidery machine and the designs available, that marking and placement are extremely important for the completion of a successful project.

Most embroidery machines have both large and small hoops available. With these hoops comes a *gridded template* to be used for proper design placement. But before you can place the design on the garment, you need to know its dimensions and the starting point for stitching. It is recommended that you trace the design onto the template with the special marking pencil provided with the machine. Line up the template with the design illustration that comes with the embroidery card making sure all registration points are accurate. The template usually will have a small hole or mark indicating the starting point for stitching.

Once you have traced your design, you can now transfer the marks to your fabric for design placement. *Air- or water-soluble marking pens or chalk* work best. Obviously, it is easiest to embroider on a flat piece of fabric, so first, lightly trace the pattern piece onto the fabric leaving additional fabric around the edges, if necessary, for hooping. Place the template on the fabric in the desired location and mark the starting point and the outer dimensions of the design. You will need the outer points if you are combining a number of designs together.

Hooping

Once you have marked completely, it is time to hoop the fabric. Place the base of the hoop on a flat surface. Cover it with the appropriate stabilizer and fabric. With the marked template resting in the inner hoop, center it over your fabric, lining up the starting points. Push the two sections of the hoop together. Many embroiderers recommend loosening the screw on the outer hoop just enough so that the inner hoop slides in place over the fabric and stabilizer.

The fabric should be held in the hoop taut but not pulled off grain or out of shape. Always pull the fabric at the same time from opposite sides to avoid distortion. If your hoop is made in such a manner, push the inner hoop slightly through the outer hoop to the back side. Attach the hoop to your machine and begin stitching, remembering to add any extra stabilizer underneath if necessary.

Be sure to read all the information provided with the various types of stabilizers before marking and hooping. Each product will have its own individual features that may need to be addressed before using.

Fabric Selection — Good and Bad

It is easy to say that you can embroider on any type of fabric, and in fact, you can—some may just take more testing than others. You will find that the more you test, the more you will learn and possibly prevent a "challenge" from happening the next time. Putting together the right combination of thread, needle, and stabilizer with your fabric and then adding proper hooping should ensure great results with practice.

But as a beginner, there are a few fabrics that will immediately cause a smile to appear on your face once you have finished the embroidery. Any medium-weight woven fabric, if stabilized properly, should be easy to stitch on. Cotton broadcloth, oxford cloth, denim, or firm wool flannels are a few types of fabrics to practice on.

Light-weight fabrics such as, silk, linen, satin, or any of the microfibers will present different challenges. A smaller needle and possibly a lighter-weight thread should be tried along with the proper stabilizer(s). Experiment for the best results.

Fabrics such as velvet, corduroy, suede, and terry cloth have a nap and are stabilized differently. Check for any hoop marks before stitching on your finished project.

Other heavy-weight fabrics, such as canvas or heavy denim, need a larger needle and possibly heavier 30 wt. rayon thread.

And knits possess different characteristics altogether. A ballpoint needle, a firmer stabilizer, and careful hooping will ensure success with knits.

Don't be afraid to experiment and test. You should be having fun with the stitching!

DESIGNER PROJECTS

SPECIAL FOR THE HOLIDAYS

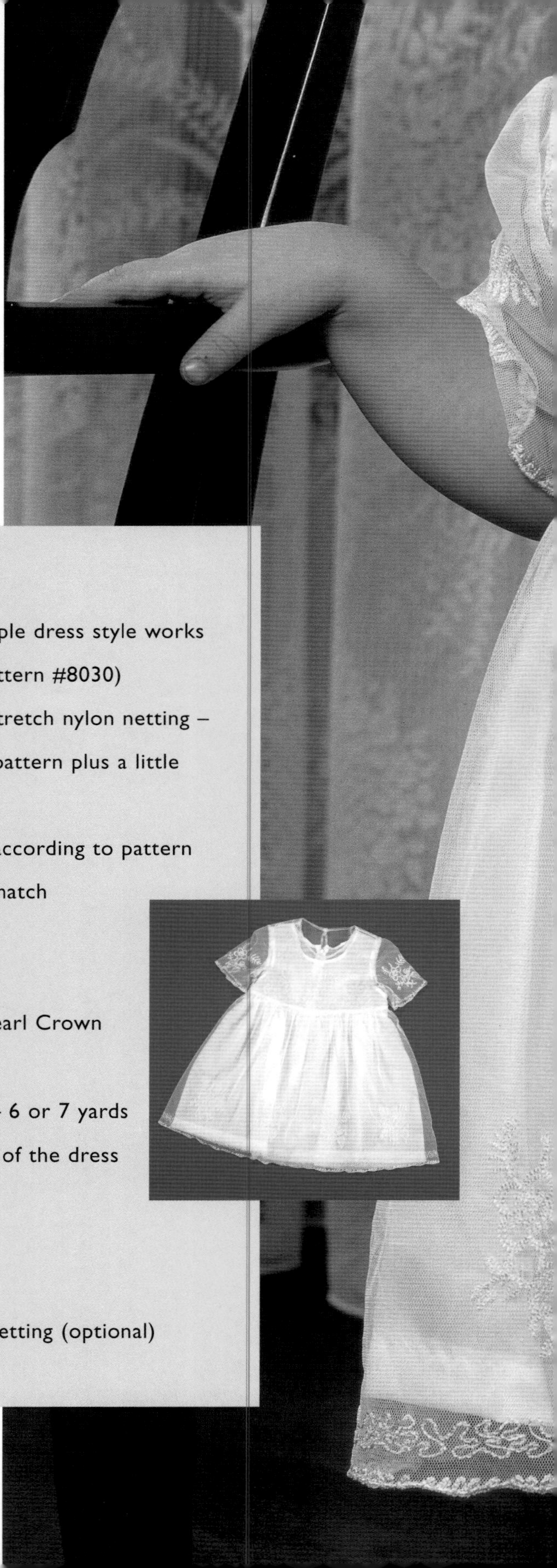

Snez Babic, Canada

*"Delicate embroidery on
fine cotton netting is
the perfect combination
for special-occasion
dressing—ideal for
any little girl."*

Sewing Supplies

Pattern of choice – a simple dress style works
    well (e,g, Simplicity pattern #8030)

English netting, tulle, or stretch nylon netting –
    yardage according to pattern plus a little
    more for hooping

Lining for slip – yardage according to pattern

50 wt. cotton thread to match

40 wt. rayon thread

Bobbin thread

Silk topstitching or YLI Pearl Crown
    Rayon thread

Water-soluble stabilizer – 6 or 7 yards
    depending on the size of the dress

Zipper

2 snaps

Edge-joining foot

Serger thread to match netting (optional)

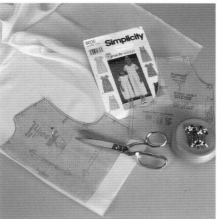

1 Cut out the dress bodice front, back, and skirt from the lining fabric. Cut three 1¼″-wide bias strips from the lining fabric. One is for the neckline and the other two strips are for the armholes.

2 Mark the dress bodice front and back pieces and the sleeves on your netting fabric. Cut out each section as a square large enough to hoop for the embroidery. Cut the skirt pieces about 4″ wider and 6″ longer than necessary. Mark the fold line for the hem on the skirt pieces.

3 Fold the water-soluble stabilizer in half along the width and press the two layers together. Cut strips from the stabilizer as necessary to embroider the dress pieces. (Snez used one large strip of the stabilizer for the skirt and cut individual strips for the bodice and sleeves.)

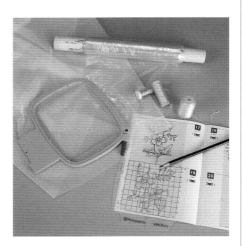

4 Thread the machine with the 40 wt. rayon thread and place the bobbin thread on the bobbin. Select an embroidery design for across the main section of the skirt pieces. Starting with one skirt piece and using your embroidery template, position the design 2" above the marked hemline. Place the netting and the water-soluble stabilizer in the hoop trying not to stretch the netting as you hoop.

5 Stitch over the design twice in the same place. Position the next design 2" above hemline, 3" from

the first design, and again, stitch twice. Continue this procedure all around the skirt pieces.

6 Hoop and stitch the embroidery design on the bodice pieces. (Snez stitched five designs on the front and two on each of the back pieces.)

7 For the sleeves, position the embroidery design slightly toward the front so that it is visible when the dress is worn. Stitch.

8 Cut away as much of the water-soluble stabilizer as you can. Sew or serge the skirt pieces together so that you have one piece.

9 Thread your machine with the 50 wt. cotton thread and place the

silk topstitching thread in the bobbin. Be sure to bypass the bobbin thread tension as directed in your instruction manual. Select a decorative stitch that is scalloped along the edge. Do not use a satin stitch as it is too dense for this type of decorative stitching. (Snez used stitch M8 on the Husqvarna Viking Designer 1; this stitch can also be found on Cassette F, #24 for other models.)

Stitch from the wrong side of the fabric with the water-soluble stabilizer on top along the hemline on the skirt. Stitch in the same manner along the hemline on each sleeve piece. Be sure to test stitches on scrap fabric first.

10 Choose a second decorative stitch and stitch above the hemline on the skirt only. (Snez used stitch E24, the stipple stitch, on the Designer 1.) You can stitch one or more rows of decorative stitches to fill in the space between the embroidery designs and the hemline on the skirt.

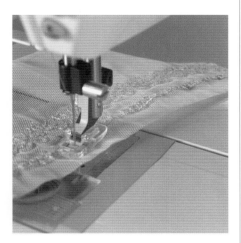

11 Select a 2.5mm-wide satin stitch. Thread the machine with the 40 wt. rayon thread and place the bobbin thread on the bobbin. Satin-stitch over the lower edge of the decorative stitch following the curves of the scallop stitch. Repeat this on the sleeves.

12 Once you have finished all of the decorative stitching, cut away as much of the water-soluble stabilizer as you can. Wash away the rest of the stabilizer leaving the fabric soft. Using a press

cloth, press with a medium-heat iron all of the dress pieces. With embroidery scissors, cut away the extra fabric from the skirt and sleeve hemlines.

13 Sew the dress pieces together according to the instructions given in your pattern. Do not insert a zipper in the dress; save it for the slip. Fold the center back seam edges under ¼" twice and topstitch. NOTE: Place a strip of water-soluble stabilizer under the netting to make topstitching easier. Fold the neckline edge under the same as for the center back seams and topstitch as above. Sew a snap at the neck edge and one at the waistline to complete the dress.

14 Sew the lining pieces together according to the instructions given in your pattern, including the zipper and hem.

15 Trim the seam allowance to ¼" at the armholes and neck edge on the lining. Press under ¼" along one long edge on each of the bias strips. Sew a bias strip to

each armhole and the neck edge using a ¼" seam. Start and stop at the side seam on the armholes and the back neck edge. Sew the bias strip ends together at the armholes and trim any excess fabric. Press to the back and pin in place.

16 At the neck back edges, fold the bias strip back in half and sew the edges closed. Trim excess fabric and press to the back; pin in place. Stitch-in-the-ditch to secure the binding. The edge-joining foot makes stitching-in-the-ditch easy.

Embroidery Equipment Used

Embroidery card #31, design 18

Husqvarna Viking Designer 1, #1+, and Rose

Husqvarna Huskylock (optional)

SLEEP TIGHT

Snez Babic, Canada

Sewing Supplies

Two purchased white pillowcases

White cotton or polyester
thread

Red 40 wt. rayon thread

Bobbin thread

Tear-away stabilizer

Serger thread to match
pillowcases (optional)

1 To prepare the pillowcases for embroidery, remove the bands. Do this carefully as each of the pieces will be reused. Open the side seam and fold each pillowcase in half lengthwise and then again into quarters. Press lightly to mark the center.

2 Thread your machine with the red rayon thread and place the bobbin thread on the bobbin. Select an appropriate outline embroidery design that will duplicate a "Redwork" effect. (Snez chose design 1 and 2 from her embroidery card.)

3 Use your embroidery template to position embroidery design in the center of one pillowcase. Hoop the fabric and the tear-away stabilizer together and embroider

the design. Repeat the procedure with the other design on the other pillowcase. Be sure to place one design on one side of one pillowcase and the other design on the other side of the second pillowcase. When the pillowcases are sitting on the bed, the open ends should be at the sides of the bed.

4 Select an embroidery design that will surround the center design like a wreath.

5 Stitch out each design moving the hoop according to your design. (Designs 25, 26, 27, and 28 were used. With the Husqvarna Standard Hoop, you will need to hoop four times. If you use the Husqvarna Plus Hoop, you need to hoop only twice—stitch design 25 in position 1 and design 26 in position 3. Stitch designs 27 and

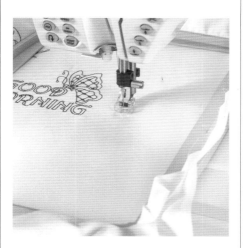

28 in the same way on the second pillowcase. Designer 1 owners can use the built-in Customizing function to customize each complete design to stitch out in the large hoop.)

6 Press open the bands. Center and stitch a border design lengthwise on one-half of one band, repeat with the other band. (Snez chose design 34 from

embroidery card #31. NOTE: To eliminate hooping a second time, baste the two bands together and hoop so that both stitching areas are in the hoop at the same time. Using the Customizing feature, stitch in one band and then the other, remembering to mirror the design.)

7 Remove the tear-away stabilizer and press all the pieces. Sew the side seam and attach the embroidered bands to finish.

Embroidery Equipment Used

Husqvarna Viking Embroidery
    card #31, designs 1, 2, 25, 26,
    27, 28, and 34

Husqvarna Viking Designer 1,
    #1+, and Rose

Husqvarna Huskylock (optional)

HORTENCE
WEARS HER HAT
TO THE SEW-IN

elinor peace bailey, United States

"Express your own

personality through this

handy scissors and needle

case. Make more than one

for all your sewing

moods."

Sewing Supplies

1 fat quarter of hand-dyed 100%
   woven cotton for head, body
   appliqué, and arms

1/4 yard of 100% cotton for bodice
   appliqué and lining of head bag

1/4 yard of fabric for hat appliqué and
   scissors case

1/4 yard of felt for glove needle cases

1 1/4" x 32" strip of 100% cotton
   for neck strap

Tear-away stabilizer

40 wt. rayon thread

Bobbin thread

Polyester fiberfill

2 upholstery rings

Turning tool

1 Stabilize a piece of hand-dyed cotton to be used for the face. Hoop your fabric and stitch out the design in the colors of your choice. Carefully remove the stabilizer from the back. (The design chosen was from Husqvarna Viking embroidery card #19.)

2 Place the embroidered face over the head pattern on a light box or up to a window to match the face placement. Trace the pattern including all markings around the face and cut out. Cut the back of the head and the chin gusset from the same fabric.

STAY STITCH
FRONT +
BACK

3 Cut two hat appliqués from the scrap fabric and pin in place, matching the markings on the embroidered face. Staystitch both front and back appliqués in place. Satin-stitch over the raw edge next to the face.

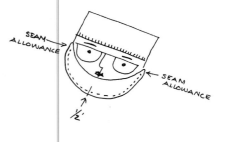

SEAM ALLOWANCE

SEAM ALLOWANCE

½"

4 Divide the chin gusset in half and center under the chin. Stitch the gusset to the face with a ¼" seam allowance, leaving ¼" at each end.

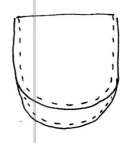

5 With right sides together, stitch the back of the head in place to the face and chin gusset.

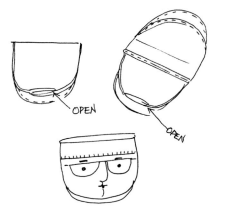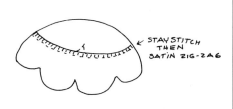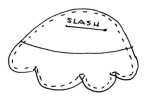

6 Cut the lining for the head bag, which includes the head front, back, and chin gusset. With right sides together, assemble the lining as you did the head, leaving 1½″ open at the chin for turning. With right sides together, stitch the flat edge of the top of the head to the same edge of the lining. Turn through the chin opening. Slipstitch the opening closed and place the lining in the head bag.

7 Cut one bodice appliqué and two full body/bodice pieces from the pattern, including all markings. Staystitch the appliqué to one body/bodice piece and cover the top raw edge with a satin stitch as before. Outline the decolletage with a straight stitch as marked.

8 With right sides together, stitch the body/bodice pieces together with a ¼″ seam allowance. Slash the fabric as indicated on the back piece. Clip, turn, and stuff softly with fiberfill. Tack the head bag over the body/bodice along the top edge.

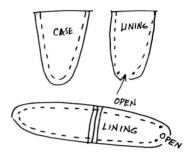

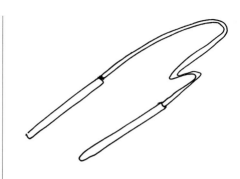

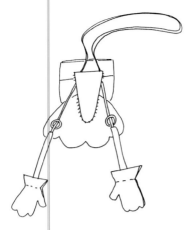

9 Cut out the scissors case and lining. With right sides together, sew the lining and the case pieces together separately, leaving an opening in the bottom of the lining for turning. With right sides together, stitch the case to the lining along the top edge. Turn through the opening and slipstitch closed. Tack the scissors case to the back of the head bag as shown in the last drawing.

10 Cut the neck strap and, with right sides together, fold the fabric in half lengthwise. Turn in one end and stitch the length, turning the tube with your turning tool.

11 Cut two arms 1¼" x 9½" from the appropriate fabric. With right sides together, fold the two pieces in half lengthwise. Stitch across one end, down the length, and turn. Stuff the arms with fiberfill and tack each arm to the end of the straps.

12 Fasten the two drapery rings as indicated on the drawing; guide the arms through the opening around the scissors case and run the arms through the rings as a guide.

13 Cut four gloves from the felt, including all markings. Topstitch along the markings for a right and left glove. Place the ends of the arms between the felt pieces and stitch across the glove cuff as indicated.

Embroidery Equipment Used

Husqvarna Viking Embroidery
   card #19, design 28

Husqvarna Viking Designer 1, #1+,
   and Rose

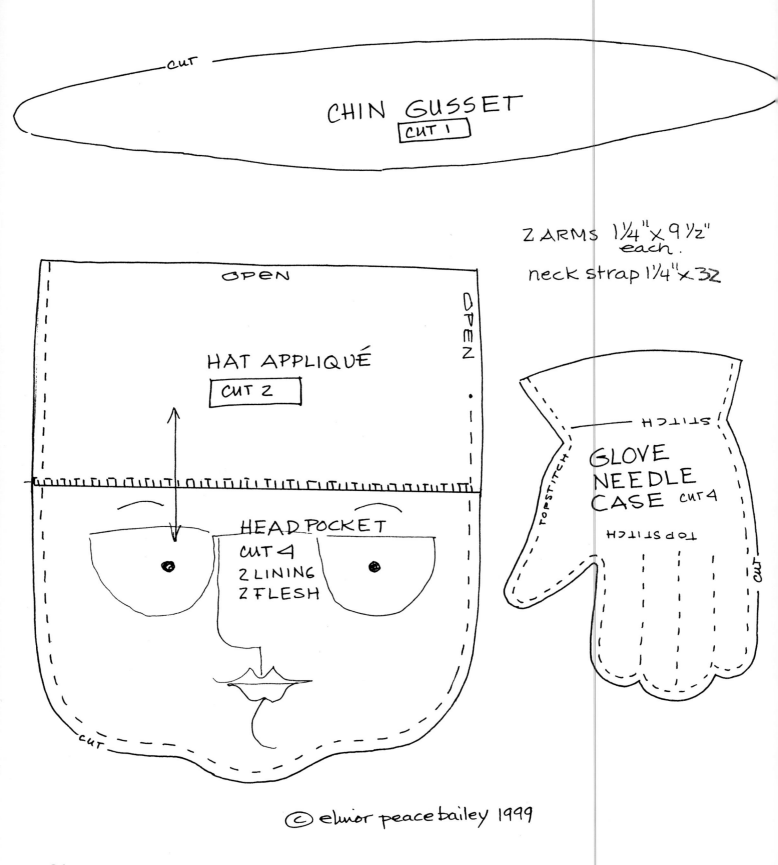

CHIN GUSSET

CUT 1

Z ARMS 1¼" x 9½" each.

neck strap 1¼" x 32

OPEN

OPEN

HAT APPLIQUÉ

CUT 2

GLOVE NEEDLE CASE CUT 4

TOPSTITCH

STITCH

TOPSTITCH

CUT

HEAD POCKET

CUT 4
2 LINING
2 FLESH

CUT

© elinor peace bailey 1999

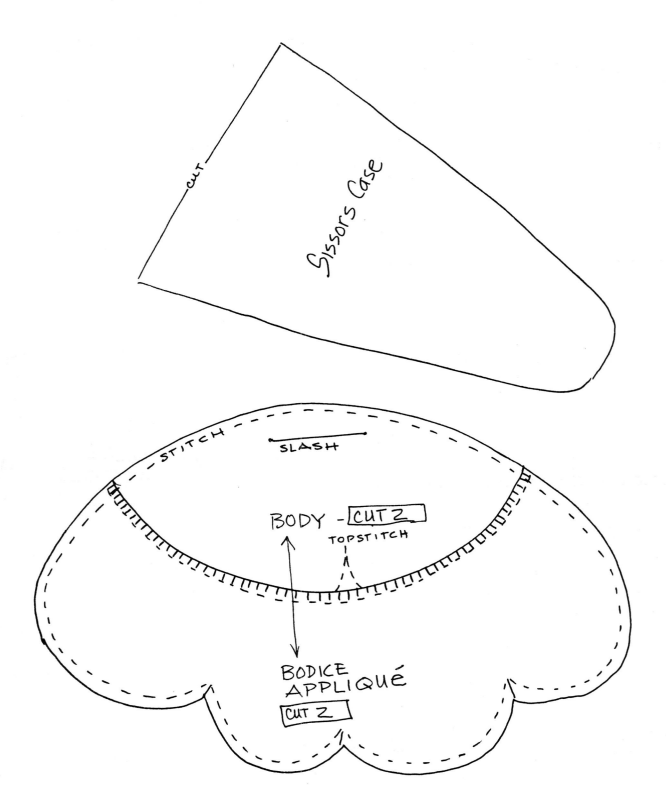

CUT

Sissors Case

STITCH

SLASH

BODY - CUT 2

TOPSTITCH

BODICE
APPLIQUÉ

CUT 2

© elinor peace bailey 1999.

EDNA LOOKING HER VERY BEST

elinor peace bailey,

United States

"Remind you of someone you know? Doll people put their personalities into their work."

Sewing Supplies

1 fat quarter of hand-dyed 100% woven cotton fabric for embroidered face

Several multicolored squares of felt for hat, purse, gloves, and hat embellishment

$1/8$ yard of cotton fabric for shoes

$1/8$ yard of cotton fabric for dress

Scrap fabrics for hair and scarf

40 wt. rayon thread

Bobbin thread

Tear-away stabilizer

Chalk or air-soluble marking pen

4 - $1/4''$ buttons for shoes

Beads for earrings and purse

Button, carpet, or craft thread

Polyester fiberfill batting

Hand-sewing needles - 3″ doll maker's, #7 darner

Crayon to enhance face

1 Lightly trace the face pattern onto the fat quarter for embroidery. Stabilize the fabric and place in the small hoop. Embroider the facial features and glasses, changing the thread colors as you desire. (Embroidery design 2 from the Husqvarna Viking embroidery card #19 was chosen. Use a design appropriate to your machine.)

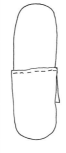

2 Cut out the face pattern adding any markings necessary. With right sides together, stitch the fabric scraps to the face using a ¼″ seam allowance at the markings for the hair. Press the pieces back and trim to the pattern size. Cut a top hairpiece using the pattern. With right sides together, stitch across the top face edge. Press up and staystitch the layers around all edges. (NOTE: All seam allowances are ¼″.)

3 Cut one face back using the pattern including the top hair, and cut one hair back from the back hairline to the top. With right sides together, stitch the back hair to the back face piece at the marks. Press the hairpiece up and staystitch. You now have completed front and back face sections.

4 Cut two pieces for the front and back dress sections and four pieces for the coat flaps using the pattern. Cut two pieces for the front and back scarf sections as well as a strip 4″ x 8″ for scarf tails and knot.

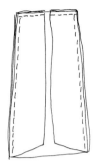

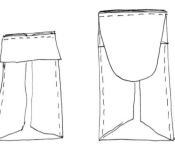

5 With right sides together, stitch the coat flaps across the bottom edge and one side. Trim the corners, turn, and press. Place the flaps on top of the front dress section and match the raw edges. Staystitch across the top and sides.

6 Stitch the scarf sections to the front and back of dress, with right sides together, matching the stitching lines. Press scarf pieces up. Staystitch the top edges. Stitch the dress sections to the face sections for both the front and back. Press the seams to one side. On the front and back sections, stitch a scallop stitch along the top scarf edge between the face and the scarf.

7 Place the front and back sections with right sides together. Stitch around all edges leaving a 1½″ opening along the bottom for turning. Clip the curve, trim the corners, and turn to the right side. Stuff the body with fiberfill batting.

8 Cut two shoe pieces using the pattern, placing the fabric on the fold. With right sides together, stitch the open edges, leaving the top open. Stuff the shoes with fiberfill.

9 Place the shoes into the opening at the bottom of the dress and slipstitch the opening closed securing the shoes in place. Add colorful buttons to the front of the shoes.

10 Cut four sleeve/arm sections from the appropriate fabric. With right sides together, stitch two sleeve/arm sections together, leaving an opening at the bottom on each. Clip the curve, trim the corners, and turn. Stuff each sleeve/arm with fiberfill and slipstitch the opening closed.

11 Cut four glove pieces from the felt, transferring all markings. Create a right and left glove by topstitching following the marks.

12 Tack the gloves to the end of each sleeve with a ladder stitch (a basic over and under stitch).

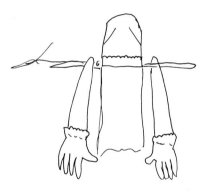

13 Line up the completed sleeves/arms on each side of the completed body. Form a colonial knot to begin using your doll needle. Enter the body from one side, exiting on the other side at the point where the sleeve will be attached.

14 Pull the thread until the tail disappears into the body. Now take a tiny stitch into the body.forming a loop. Bring the needle through the loop and back through the new loop making a figure eight. Pull gently to tighten the thread. Stitch the arms to the body using a sheepshank. (A sheepshank requires you to wrap the thread as you would for a button shank.) Pass the needle through the top of the arm section and then back through toward the body. Wrap the thread forming a loop, pass the needle through the loop and pull tight. Repeat on each side making sure the sleeves/arms are secure.

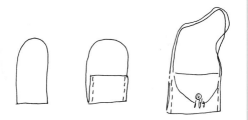 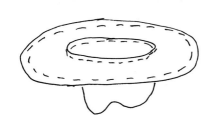 

15 Cut the purse and a ½" x 10" strap from the felt. Fold the bottom section of the purse up and stitch along each side. Tack the strap ends to each side of the purse. Add beads or other embellishments to the purse flap. Place the strap in the glove and turn up the fingers and tack to hold.

16 Cut two hat brims and two hat crowns from felt. Stitch the crown sections together leaving the bottom open. Clip and turn. Stitch the brim sections together around the other edge and cut out the inner section. Clip and turn. Place the crown section into the brim section and stitch together. Topstitch the outer edge of the brim. Place the hat on the doll's head and tack invisibly.

17 Fold the scarf piece in half lengthwise. Stitch leaving a small opening for turning. Trim the corners and turn; press. Knot in the center and tack the scarf to the neckline

18 Use your crayons to enhance the facial features, adding rouge or eye shadow. Add earrings to each side of the head.

Embroidery Equipment Used

Husqvarna Viking Embroidery
card #19, design 2

Husqvarna Viking Designer 1, #1+,
and Rose

Edna Looking Her Very Best

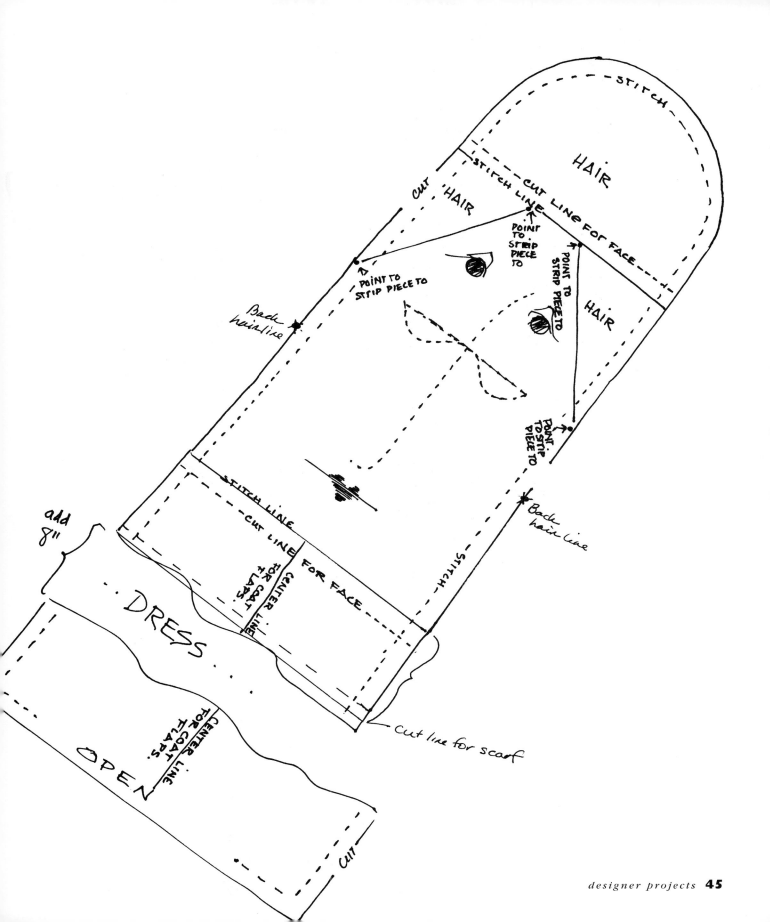

STITCH

HAIR

CUT

STITCH LINE

CUT LINE FOR FACE

'HAIR'

POINT TO STRIP PIECE TO

POINT TO STRIP PIECE TO

POINT TO STRIP PIECE TO

Back hairline

HAIR

POINT TO STRIP PIECE TO

Back hair line

add 8"

STITCH LINE

CUT LINE FOR COAT FLAPS.

CENTER LINE

CUT LINE FOR FACE

STITCH

DRESS

cut line for scarf

CENTER LINE FOR COAT FLAPS.

OPEN

CUT

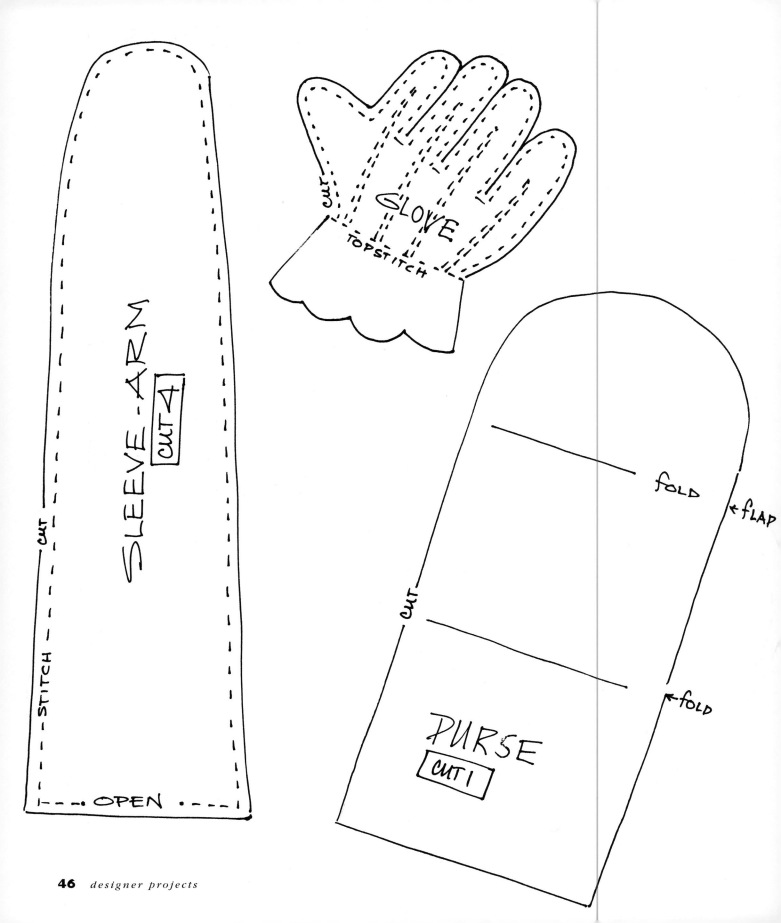

CUT

STITCH

SLEEVE ARM
CUT 4

OPEN

GLOVE

CUT

TOPSTITCH

fold

← flap

CUT

← fold

PURSE
CUT 1

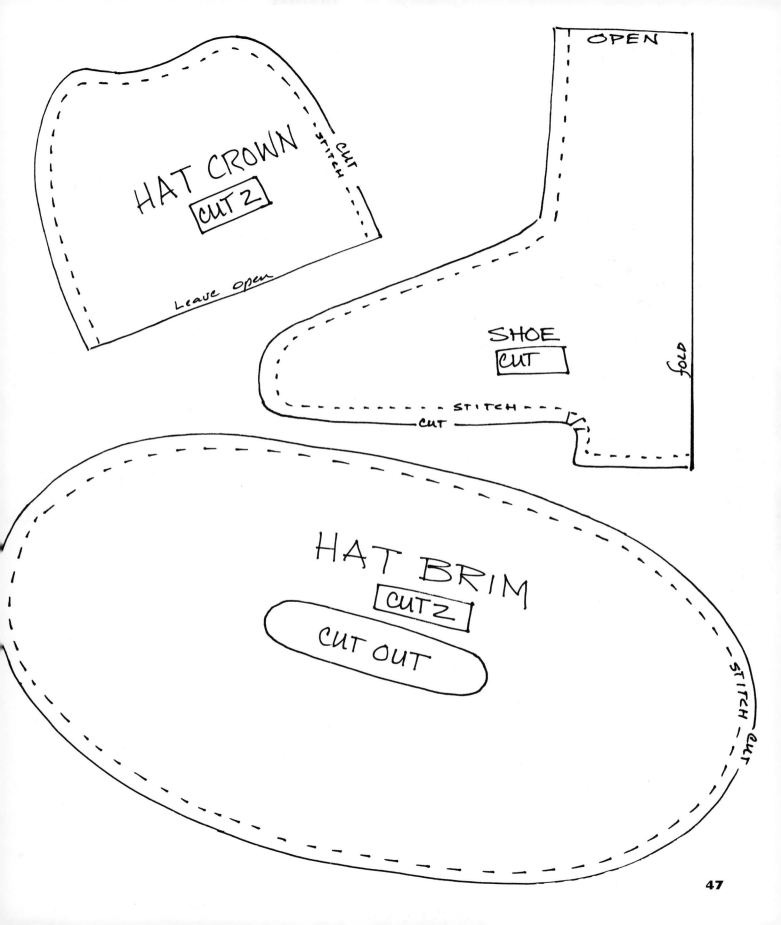

HAT CROWN
CUT 2

STITCH
CUT
Leave open

OPEN

FOLD

SHOE
CUT

STITCH
CUT

HAT BRIM
CUT 2
CUT OUT

STITCH OUT

47

SHORT AND SASSY

Carola Boberg, Sweden

"Duplicate the embroidery ideas you are seeing in ready-to-wear easily on your sewing mahine. Couture designs are at your fingertips."

Sewing Supplies

Pattern of choice (e.g. Burda #2735)

Linen fabric - yardage according to pattern

40 wt. rayon thread in monochromatic
   tones

Bobbin thread

1 skirt zipper

Tear-away stabilizer

Air- or water-soluble marking pen

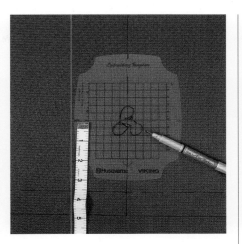

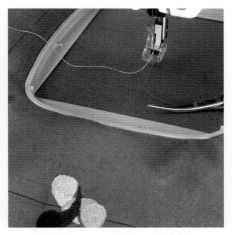

1 Lightly trace the skirt front and back onto the linen fabric with a marking pen. Cut around the fabric leaving extra fabric along the edges. Mark the hemline on both front and back pieces.

2 Mark the design placement approximately 3″ (7.5cm) from the finished bottom edge (hemline) in the center front and back. (Carola selected design 13 from Husqvarna Viking embroidery card #33. You can choose a similar geometric design for your

machine or create the embroidery motif using the free-motion techniques.)

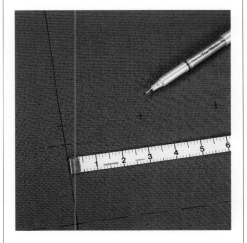

3 Leaving 3¼″ (8 cm) between designs, mark the placement on either side of the center using your embroidery template.

4 Using the largest hoop, place tear-away stabilizer under your fabric and stitch out the designs

on the front and back skirt sections. (NOTE: The 240 x 150 hoop allows three designs to be sewn without re-hooping.) There are five motifs stitched across the front and back pieces.

5 Once all the embroidery is completed, remove the stabilizer and cut out the skirt pieces. Finish according to the pattern instructions.

Embroidery Equipment Used

Husqvarna Viking Embroidery
   card #33, design 13
Husqvarna Viking Designer 1,
   #1+, and Rose

FUN IN THE SUN

Carola Boberg, Sweden

Sewing Supplies

Pattern of choice (e.g. Burda #3029)

Cotton fabric – yardage according
   to pattern

40 wt. rayon thread

Bobbin thread

3 buttons

Purchased pre-folded bias binding

Air- or water-soluble marking pen

Tear-away stabilizer

1 Trace the back bodice pattern pieces onto your fabric with an air- or water-soluble marking pen. Cut around the pieces leaving extra fabric for hooping.

2 Mark the placement for the flowers in a vertical line for the center back.

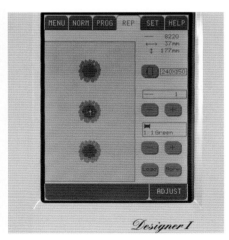

3 Using a large hoop, place the

tear-away stabilizer under the fabric and stitch out the designs. (This complete motif was achieved by using the built-in Customizing feature and the 240 x 150 hoop on the Husqvarna Viking Designer 1 to stitch out three designs in a row.)

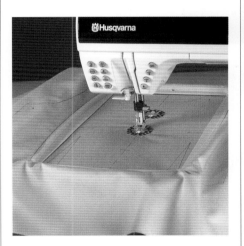

4 Stitch out the designs. For the flowers on the front of the dress, use a small hoop to hold your fabric. Remove all the stabilizer once the stitching is completed.

5 Check your pattern pieces against the traced lines and cut out the bodice sections, eliminating the seam allowances at the neck and armhole edges

and any hem allowance. Do not cut out any facings for the neck edge or armholes.

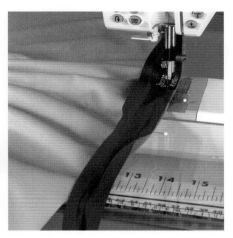

6 Open out the pre-folded bias tape. Using the pressed channel as your guide, match the raw edges and stitch the tape to the neck edge, armholes, and bottom hemline from the wrong side.

7 Fold the binding over the raw edge and stitch the bias tape in place from the right side.

Embroidery Equipment Used
Husqvarna Viking Embroidery
    card #33, design 22
Husqvarna Viking Designer 1,
    #1+, and Rose

SUMMER DENIM

Terry Fox, Great Britian

"A shift dress makes a wonderful backdrop for all embroidery designs. You can add as little or as much as you like... A good tip is to concentrate in one particular area at a time. After all, you may decide that is enough, especially if time runs out. So although I believe in total freedom as you work, some thought has to be given to the overall balance of the design. The front of my dress appears to be embroidered at random. But the panel has actually been split into four sections so I could stop at any point."

Sewing Supplies

Pattern of choice (preferably with darts and center back seam but not a Princess line)

Fabric – yardage according to the pattern

40 wt. rayon thread

Bobbin thread

Lightweight stabilizer

Air- or water-soluble marking pen

1 Place the front and back pattern pieces on the fabric. Using a colored thread or a water-soluble marking pen, outline all of the seams and darts. Cut out the panels leaving extra fabric on all sides for hooping.

2 Draw the guidelines for your motif placement onto the fabric, deciding where you want to place the flower embroideries. Divide the space into sections for easier placement. Five motifs were chosen for this dress. (Terry used designs 31, 32, 33, 34, and 35 from embroidery card #23 on the Husqvarna Viking #1+, or you can choose a similar design for your machine.)

3 Hoop and stabilize the fabric. Stitch the designs in various sizes or select only certain sections of the design to sew out—for instance, use only the leaves from a certain design. Be prepared to stop the machine when the portion of the design is completed if it is not a programmed color change.

4 Once all the motifs are sewn, join them together with a satin stitch following your original design lines. Vary the stitch width at times to add interest.

5 Complete the back section in the same manner as the front. Add any additional highlights between the flowers on both the back and front. (Terry selected embroidery designs 11, 12, and 30 from card #23.) Now the embroidery is complete.

6 Compare your pattern pieces according to your size. Add ⅜" to the center back seam making the zipper seam allowance 1" wide and cut out all pieces.

7 Stitch your bust and front and back waist darts if any. Stitch the shoulder seams on the dress and the facings.

8 Press the center back seam to the wrong side. (NOTE: The center back seam is not sewn at this point.)

9 With right sides up, on the left side of the dress, clip the neck edge ½" from the seam allowance fold and down ⅝". Open out the seam allowance and fold down the section between the clips. Fold back the seam allowance and press.

10 With right sides together, pin the facing to the dress. Stitch around the armholes and the neckline as far as the center back on both sides. Clip the curves and trim the seam to ⅛".

11 With your hand inside the facing through the shoulder seam, pull the back section through to the front. Repeat on the other side. Press all seams.

Terry's Cheat Zipper

12 With a diagonal cut, snip into the seam allowance on the center back seam to the bottom point of the zipper. Press the seam above the clip to the wrong side.

13 Topstitch along the center back fold from the top, pivot at the bottom, and finish at the bottom zipper clip. Press. (NOTE: The snip at the neckline should still be neatly tucked to the wrong side.)

14 With right sides together, pin the center back seams from the clip down. Stitch to the clip. Press the seam open.

15 Place the zipper under the right-hand side, teeth against the fold. Stitch along the fold line from top to bottom with your zipper foot.

16 Bring over the center seams to match. Pin along the topstitched line on the left-hand side through to the zipper

17 Lift up the left-hand side to reveal the seam. You can feel the pins through the fabric. Stitch as close to the zipper as possible on the wrong side from bottom to top.

18 With right sides together, pin the side seams, opening out the facings. Stitch both side seams, clip, and press open. Hem as desired.

Embroidery Equipment Used
Husqvarna Viking Embroidery card #23, designs 11, 12, 30, 31, 32, 33, 34, and 35
Husqvarna Viking Designer 1, #1+, and Rose

FOR AN ANGEL

Terry Fox, Great Britian

"If I was five years old, this
would be my dream top. In fact, I
did think about making a larger
one for myself, but after showing
my husband and asking 'what do
you think', well, I'm afraid the
look said it all!"

Sewing Supplies

Pattern of choice (simple pullover
   top preferred)
Fabric — yardage according to
   pattern (sequined fabric used
   here)
Fine, fusible interfacing
Organza, and wash-away and tear-
   away stabilizers for embroideries
1/4 yard of lining fabric
Embroidery floss and needle
40 wt. rayon thread
Bobbin thread

A
pocket full of
secrets

1 Following the pattern instructions, stitch the shoulder seams, attach the facings, and finish the neckline edge, and press. Turn to the right side.

2 To prepare the pocket, make a cardboard template of the finished size. Trace the pocket on the fabric and cut a piece large enough to fit into the hoop, allowing for ⅝″ seam allowances and a 1¼″ facing at the top.

3 Stabilize as necessary and hoop. For more delicate fabrics, use the basting feature and baste the fabric to the stabilizer prior to adding the embroidery.

4 Stitch the motif in the middle. (Terry chose design 7 from embroidery card #23 on the Husqvarna Viking #1+, or you can select a similar design on your machine.)

5 Once the design is stitched, remove from the machine but not from the hoop. Using your marking pen, write in freehand, 'A pocket full of secrets' around the motif.

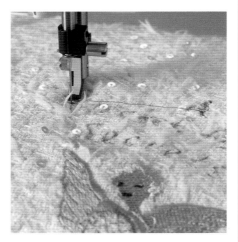

6 Using a narrow zig zag or straight stitch, fill in the letters with freehand embroidery.

7 Add three or four bullion roses around the face of the cherub.

8 Cut a piece of interfacing the size of the cardboard pocket template. Adhere to the wrong side of the embroidery, matching the traced line. Cut out the pocket adding ⅝″ seam allowances on the sides and 1¼″ facing across the top.

9 Cut a square of lining slightly larger than the pocket. Stitch the lining to the pocket facing edge with right sides together. Press the seam open.

10 Bring the lining over the pocket; press along the fold line. Cut the lining to the same size as the embroidered fabric.

11 Open out the pocket and place wrong side up on the ironing board. Position the cardboard template on the pocket and press the seams to the wrong side. Trim the seam allowance to ⅜″ and remove the cardboard template.

12 Trim ⅛″ from the sides (not the top) of the cardboard template. Lay the trimmed template on the lining side of the pocket with the top edge against the top fold. Draw the template, transferring the shape of the pocket to the lining.

13 Place the lining side of the pocket to the garment right sides together. Pin in place. Mark a point ½″ in along the fold line on either side of the pocket.

14 Stitch in place from one marked point around the pocket to the opposite side. Press the lining in along the stitched line; trim.

15 Bring the embroidered pocket section down over the top and slipstitch the edges to secure.

16 Complete the top according to the pattern instructions.

17 To stitch the dangling angels, select 5 designs (The designs may be mirror-imaged—designs 1, 2, and 21 from embroidery card #23.)

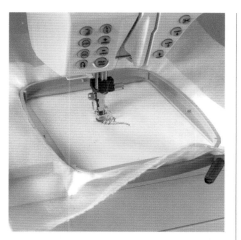

18 Layer organza and heavier tear-away stabilizer in the hoop. Stitch out each design and carefully cut out close to the edge.

19 Stitch out a number of separate motifs using organza and a lighter weight wash- or tear-away stabilizer. This will keep the motifs lighter and not as thick as the ones attached to the hem. (Terry used designs 1, 2, 4, 21, 22, and 27 for the 'secrets' on

embroidery card #23. After trimming, place them in the pocket with just a peep showing over the top!

20 Beginning in the center of the front hem using your embroidery floss and needle, make three loops of thread from the hem to the embroidery. Form a blanket stitch over the strands of thread back to the hem. Repeat for all hanging embroideries.

Embroidery Equipment Used

Husqvarna Viking Embroidery
    card #23, designs 1, 2, 4, 7, 21,
    22, and 27

Husqvarna Viking Designer 1,
    #1+, and Rose

ELEGANT EVENINGS

Terry Fox, Great Britian

"This dress was inspired by the Oscars. I love the simplicity (of the design) with the only detail being in the back. ....

I adore cherubs and angels; they can be found in every corner of my house.

I have also secretly desired a tattoo and love designing all sorts of garments with my interpretation of them, but obviously these are far less painful. I think if I were to have one it would look something like this!"

Sewing Supplies

Pattern of choice (e.g. Vogue #1584)

Velvet fabric – yardage according to pattern

Approximately ¾–1 yard of stretch illusion fabric

Approximately ¾–1 yard of silk organza

Lining fabric – yardage according to pattern

40 wt. rayon thread

Bobbin thread

5" hook-and-eye tape or 2 sets of hooks and eyes

2 velvet butterflies

3 small sequined hearts

Silk thread

Fine hand-sewing needle

Tear-away stabilizer

1 Because the illusion fabric has such a powerful two-way stretch, the silk organza is a perfect backing but must be firmly tacked into position. Layer the illusion over the organza and pin the back bodice pattern to the layers. Baste the outline of the back panel to the fabric layers and remove the pattern. Using a very fine needle and silk thread, baste horizontal and vertical lines approximately 3"–4" apart.

2 Cut out the back bodice panel along the waist seam only and pin back the organza.

3 Stitch the velvet skirt panels together along the center back seam. Clip if necessary and press the seam open.

4 Stitch the back skirt to the back bodice along the waist seam, making sure you do not catch the organza. Trim, clip, and press the seam toward the skirt.

5 Starting on the right-hand side of the bodice, draw a slow curve toward the left-hand side of the skirt. Use your embroidery template for spacing the designs. Eight separate motifs are used for the main part of the design.

6 Following the pattern provided, start at the top and work your way down toward the hem, following the curved line. Hoop your fabric, adding a tear-away stabilizer to the back of the velvet.

7 Mirror-image the motifs as shown. Select your thread colors to create an overall theme, eliminating any colors if necessary. Stitch.

8 Add the velvet butterflies and little sequined hearts for texture and interest and to express your own personality too! Once all the embroideries are stitched, you are now ready to complete the dress.

9 Remove all of the organza from the back of the illusion fabric, being careful when cutting close to the motifs. Cut out the rest of the top bodice panel to size.

10 Turn back the seam allowance on both the back armholes and neck edge of the illusion fabric. Stitch in place using a stretch stitch. Trim the seam allowance close to the stitching line.

11 Stitch the bust darts in both the velvet and the lining; press.

12 With right sides together, pin the front lining to the front dress section around the neck and front armholes only. Stitch the seams but do not stitch the shoulder seams. Clip and trim the seam to ⅛″. Turn to the right side.

13 On one shoulder, with right sides together, pin the front shoulder to the back and stitch. Press the shoulder seam toward the front. Bring the lining over the seam tucking the seam allowance inside and slipstitch in place.

14 On the other shoulder seam, press the seam allowance to the wrong side on both the front and the back.

15 Place the hook side of the tape to the front shoulder seam and stitch in place. Repeat on the back section using the eye side of the tape.

16 Stitch the front and back sections together along the side seams. Repeat for the lining. Clip, overlock, and press all seams.

17 Pin the lining to the wrong side along the back waist and slipstitch in place.

18 Hem both the dress and the lining.

Embroidery Equipment Used
Husqvarna Viking Embroidery card #23, designs 4, 5, 6, 7, 9, 14, and 25 (see diagram)
Husqvarna Viking Designer 1, #1+, and Rose

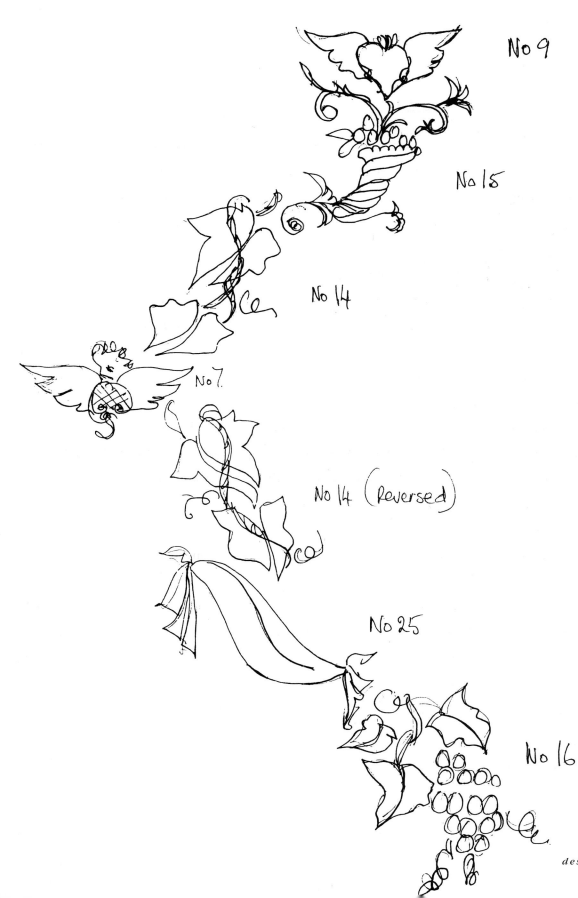

No 9

No 15

No 14

No 7

No 14 (Reversed)

No 25

No 16

FRUITS OF THE SEASON

Ingrid Larson Haglund, Sweden

Sewing Supplies

½ yard of linen for inset

¾ yard coordinating solid fabric

14″ zipper

16″ pillow form

40 wt. rayon thread

Bobbin thread

Air-soluble marking pen

1 Cut from the coordinating fabric for the pillow front, two 4½″ x 15″ rectangles and two 4½″ x 22″ rectangles. For the pillow back, cut one 22″ x 23½″ rectangle.

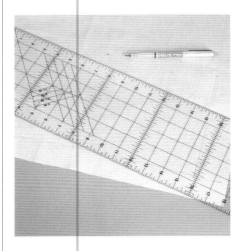

2 Mark a 15″ square on the linen for the pillow inset. (Do not cut out the square until the embroidery is complete.) Measure in 5″ from each side edge and 7½″ from the bottom and top to find the center of the embroidery designs.

3 The linen is now marked into four squares. Stitch the embroidery in each section. Turn

the fabric 180 degrees and stitch the embroidery again on the other half.

4 Stitch a monogram in the center if desired. (Palace Script lettering included with the Husqvarna Viking Designer 1 was selected. Use size 30mm and adjust the width to the largest size.) When the embroidery is complete, mark the 15″ square again and cut.

5 Using a ½″ seam allowance, with right sides together, stitch the 4½″ x 15″ rectangles to the top and bottom of the pillow inset along the long edges. Press the seam allowances toward the contrasting fabric. Stitch the 4½″ x 22″ rectangles to the sides of the inset along the other edges. Press

the seam allowance toward the contrasting fabric.

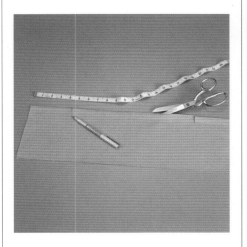

6 With right sides together, fold the large rectangle in half along the 23½″ side; press. Measure down 4½″ along the folded edge from each end and mark. Using a ¾″ seam allowance, stitch from the edge to the first mark. Backstitch then baste from mark to mark and seam again from the second mark to the opposite end. Clip into the seam and cut the

fold open between the marks. Press the seam open and insert a zipper between the marks. Press seam allowance flat at each end of zipper and remove the basting.

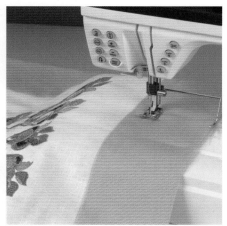

7 With right sides together, pin the pillow front to the pillow back. Using a ½″ seam allowance, stitch. Trim the seam allowances at the corners. To make a flange, use an air-soluble marker and mark in 1″ from the embroidered inset. Stitch. Insert pillow form to complete.

Embroidery Equipment Used

Husqvarna Viking Embroidery
    card #107
Husqvarna Viking Designer 1,
    #1+, and Rose

IT'S A PICNIC

Ingrid Larson Haglund, Sweden —
designed by Jean Knudsen

"The beauty of these elaborate
appliqué and embroidery designs just
invited an elegant picnic setting.
Perfect either for an evening at the
symphony or a simple family
gathering, Ingrid's designs speak for
themselves."

TABLECLOTH

Sewing Supplies

1⁵/₈ yards of primary fabric

1 yard of linen for inset

³/₈ yard of coordinating

    fabric for embroidery

    appliqué and ties

40 wt. rayon thread

Bobbin thread

Seam sealant

Air- or water-soluble

    marking pen

Turning tool

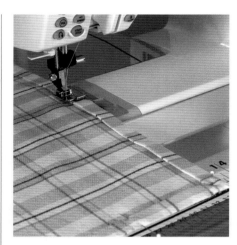

1 From the primary fabric, cut a 54″ square. Press up 1″ on all sides and fold to miter the corners. Fold in the raw edge and stitch on all sides to hem.

2 For the linen inset, pull threads to create an exact 32″ square. (NOTE: Since the linen squares are to be fringed, it is important that they be exactly on grain.) Cut out the square along the pulled-thread lines. Mark in ¾″ from the cut edge and pull the threads on this new line.

3 Select a narrow zig zag or lightening stitch on your machine and stitch along the pulled-thread line.

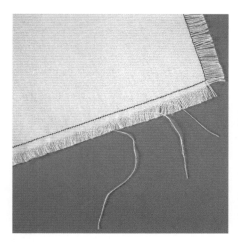

4 Fringe the square to the stitching line on all sides.

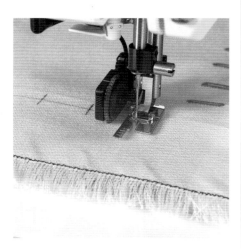

5 Beginning 3″ from each side edge and 2″ in from the fringed edge, mark ¾″-long buttonholes every inch from corner to corner. Using your buttonhole attachment, stitch equal-size buttonholes. To prevent fraying, apply seam sealant to the wrong side of the buttonholes before cutting open.

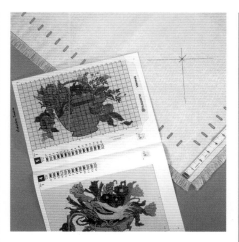

6 Measure in 7¾″ from the stitching line at each corner. Extend lines to cross. Use this point as the center for your embroidery. Select an appropriate fruit basket or bunch of fruit from your embroidery library. (Jean chose design 107 from Ingrid Larson Haglund's embroidery card #108 for the Husqvarna Viking Designer 1.) Stitch according to the embroidery prompts on your machine, changing thread colors as necessary.

7 After pressing both squares, place the linen square "on point" over the hemmed cloth. Mark a line just above the buttonholes on all sides and stitch the two pieces together.

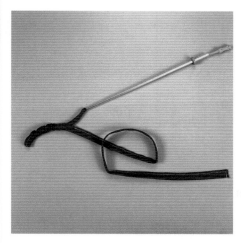

8 Cut four bias strips, ½″ x 47″, piecing where necessary. With right sides together, stitch across each end and halfway down along the long edge using a ¼″ seam allowance. Repeat from the other end leaving a 1″ opening for turning. Turn and hand-stitch opening closed. Thread strips through buttonholes from corner to corner and tie into bows.

BASKET LINER

Sewing Supplies

½ yard primary fabric

½ yard linen fabric

1½" x 52" coordinating
   fabric for tie

23" of ⅜" elastic

4" x 20" of tear-away
   stabilizer cut into
   1" x 20" strips

40 wt. rayon thread

Bobbin thread

Seam sealant

Air- or water-soluble
   marking pen

Bodkin

1 Cut from the primary fabric, one 15" diameter circle for the lining; one 33" x 7¾" piece for the top; and one 33" x 3¾" piece for the bottom facing. Pull thread on the linen fabric to create an exact 18" square. Mark in ½" and pull threads along the marked lines. Finish the square following the instructions in steps 3 and 4 for the Tablecloth, pages 68 and 69.

2 Using an air-soluble marking pen, mark 1¾" in from the stitching at each corner. Extend these lines until they intersect. Since the edges have already been finished, use an adhesive stabilizer to hold the fabric in place while stitching the embroidery. Using the marks as the center point, place your fabric in the embroidery hoop over the stabilizer and stitch an apple design on each corner.

3 Beginning ¼" in from each

corner, mark every ½". Select a medium-wide satin stitch and stitch between markings leaving a ½" space between each bar of stitching along all four edges. Use the strips of tear-away stabilizer to support the stitching.

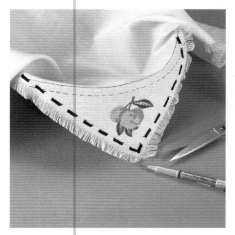

4 Lay a corner of the embroidered square along the edge of your basket and finger-press the outline into the square. Mark a dashed line along the crease for the start line. Place another line ½" from the first line. (NOTE: These lines will be slightly curved.) Cut along the solid line and use this corner to cut the other three corners.

5 With right sides together, fold the bottom facing in half along the short side. Join the ends with a ½" seam. Press the seam open

and the seam allowance edges under ¼″. Edge-stitch the seam allowance edges down.

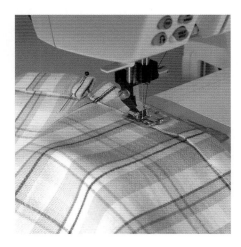

6 For the top, with right sides together, fold the larger rectangle in half along the short edge. Stitch a ½″ seam beginning 1¾″ down from the edge. Finish the seam allowance as in step 5. For the casing, press ¼″ to the wrong side along the long edge with the opening. Fold under ¾″ and press

again. Edge-stitch down close to fold.

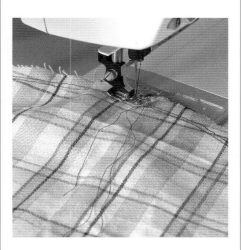

7 Stitch two rows of basting stitches around the edge of the 15″ circle. Gather the edge until the outer edge (circumference) measures 32″.

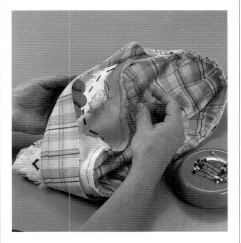

8 Pin the wrong side of the basket top to the right side of the gathered circle. Adjust the gathers to fit and baste to hold. Pin the

right side of the embroidered corners to the right side of the basket top, overlapping the fringed edges. Baste in place. Pin the right side of the basket facing to the wrong side of the basted pieces. Stitch with a ½″ seam through all the thicknesses. Zig zag over the raw edge to finish.

9 Make a tie from the coordinating fabric strip as you did for the Tablecloth, page 69. Insert the tie into the top casing with the bodkin. Insert elastic into the casing on the bottom basket facing.

INSULATED WINE
BOTTLE COVER

Sewing Supplies

1/4 yard of primary fabric

1/4 yard of linen fabric

6½" x 20" of fusible fleece

1½" x 36" coordinating

   fabric for tie

4" x 10" tear-away

   stabilizer cut into

   1" x 10" strips

40 wt. rayon thread

Bobbin thread

1 Cut two 21" x 7½" rectangles for the cover and lining and one 6¾" x 1½" rectangle for the top.

2 On the linen fabric, pull thread to create an 8" x 15" rectangle. Measure ½" from each edge and pull threads again. Stitch along pulled-thread line and fringe to stitching line as described in Tablecloth steps 3 and 4, pages 68 and 69.

3 Stabilize your fabric, and following the embroidery information on your machine, embroider the apple design as you did for the Basket Liner in step 2, page 70.

4 Add the satin stitching along the edges as you did for the Basket Liner in step 3, page 70.

5 Mark up 7" along each edge following the zig zag stitching at each corner. Connect the marks forming a triangle. Repeat at opposite corner. Cut out two triangles.

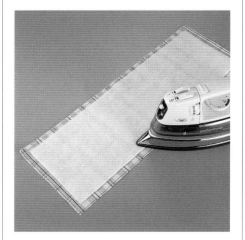

6 For the cover body, fuse the fleece following the manufacturer's instructions to the wrong side of

the primary fabric leaving ½" seam allowance around all edges.

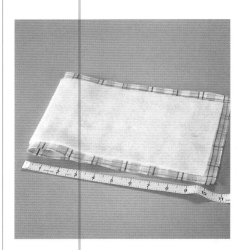

7 With right sides together, fold the fused piece in half matching the short sides. Stitch down each side stopping 2¾" from the fold.

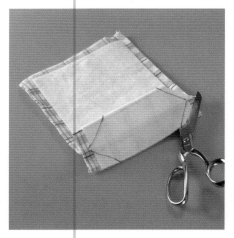

8 To create the bottom of the bag, bring the fold up to meet the stitching keeping an equal amount of fabric at each side. Stitch a

45-degree angle to the fold from the seam to the bottom folded edge. Repeat this at each corner to create a box-like bottom. Trim the corners ¼″ from the stitching.

9 For the lining, repeat steps 7 and 8, leaving a 4″ opening along one side seam.

10 For the top, with right sides together, fold the rectangle matching the short ends. Seam and finish the top as you did for the Basket Liner in step 6, page 71.

11 Assemble the cover as follows: Pin the wrong side of the embroidered corners to the right side of the bottle cover body, matching the raw edges and overlapping the fringe. Baste the pieces together to hold. With right sides together, pin the top to the body matching the raw edges; baste. With the right side of the lining to the wrong side of the top, pin the lining over the entire basted pieces matching the raw

edges. Stitch with a ½″ seam allowance and trim close to stitching. Turn the bottle cover through the opening in the side of the lining and push the lining to the inside of the cover. Slipstitch the opening closed.

NAPKINS

Sewing Supplies

For four napkins:

   1⅛ yards of linen fabric

4″ x 20″ tear-away stabilizer cut into 1″ x 20″ strips

40 wt. rayon thread

Bobbin thread

1 Make four 18″ fringed squares as you have done for the Basket Liner in step 1, page 70.

2 Mark and embroider the apple design in one corner as on the Basket Liner in step 2, page 70.

3 Satin-stitch around all the edges as on the Basket Liner in step 3, page 70.

Embroidery Equipment Used

Husqvarna Viking Embroidery
   Library design #211601 (apples)

Husqvarna Viking Embroidery
   card #107

Husqvarna Viking Designer 1,
   #1+, and Rose

12 Make a tie from the coordinating fabric strip as you did on the tablecloth. Insert the tie into the casing with the bodkin.

ELEGANT SILK BAG

Anna Haraldsson, Sweden

"This simple but elegant

bag is enhanced

with the overall

embroidery design."

Sewing Supplies

1 yard of 50"/55"-wide raw silk

10" of lining fabric

40 wt. rayon thread

Bobbin thread

Tear-away stabilizer

Turning tool

Air-soluble marking pen

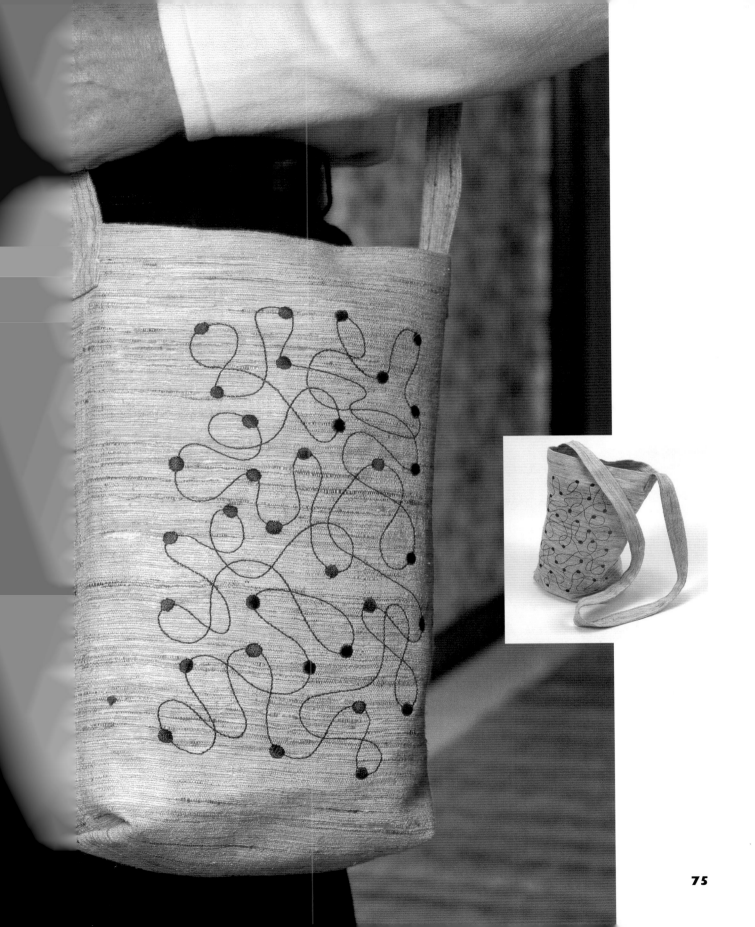

1 Cut one 12" x 32" rectangle from the silk fabric, and one 3" x 40" strip for the strap. Cut one 10" x 28" piece from the lining fabric.

2 Fold the silk rectangular piece in half lengthwise and finger-press to mark the center.

3 Measure down 8" along the creased line and mark for the embroidery.

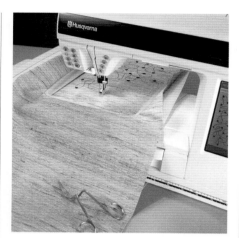

4 Layer the fabric over the tear-away stabilizer and place in the hoop. (On the Husqvarna Viking Designer 1, select design 3:1 from the embroidery card #108, or choose a comparable design for your machine.) Stitch the design according to the information given on the screen. Remove the stabilizer and press from the wrong side.

5 Centering the design, cut approximately 1" from each long side resulting in a piece 10" wide.

6 With right sides together, fold the bag in half and pin. Using a ⅜" seam allowance, sew the side seams. Press the sewn seams to one side. Finger-press a crease at the center bottom.

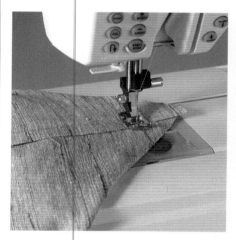

7 To create a square bottom for the bag, match the side seams and the newly finger-pressed crease, forming a triangle. Pin. Mark from the point down the seam 1½" and draw a line from edge to edge. Stitch using the line as your guide.

8 With right sides together, fold the lining piece in half and sew the side seams using a ⅜" seam allowance, leaving a 3" opening on one side.

9 Stitch box corners on the lining as described in step 7. Turn the lining right side out and press.

10 Place the lining inside the silk bag with right sides together, matching the top raw edges and side seams. Pin. Sew around the top of the bag using a ⅜" seam allowance. Press the top edge, favoring the silk fabric.

11 Turn the bag right side out through the opening in the lining. Slipstitch the opening closed.

12 Fold down the top edge 2" to the inside. Press.

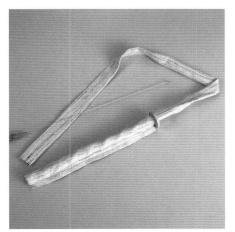

13 Fold the strap fabric in half lengthwise with right sides together. Stitch a ⅜" seam allowance along the long side. Using your turning tool, turn the strap to the right side. Press, keeping the seam to one side.

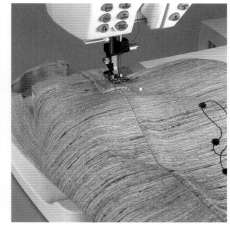

14 Fold back the raw edges on each end approximately ½". Pin the strap to the sides of the bag, centering over the side seams. Sew an X to secure.

Embroidery Equipment Used
Husqvarna Viking Embroidery card #108, design 3:1
Husqvarna Viking Designer 1, #1+, and Rose

SUBTLE EMBROIDERED GRASSES

Anna Haraldsson, Sweden

"I like it when the embroideries are embedded in the garment— not as if they had been stuck on afterwards. The embroidery should follow the lines of the garment and flatter your figure. For this blouse, I chose a pattern without many seams and darts. I placed the grass embroidery growing from the edge of the blouse."

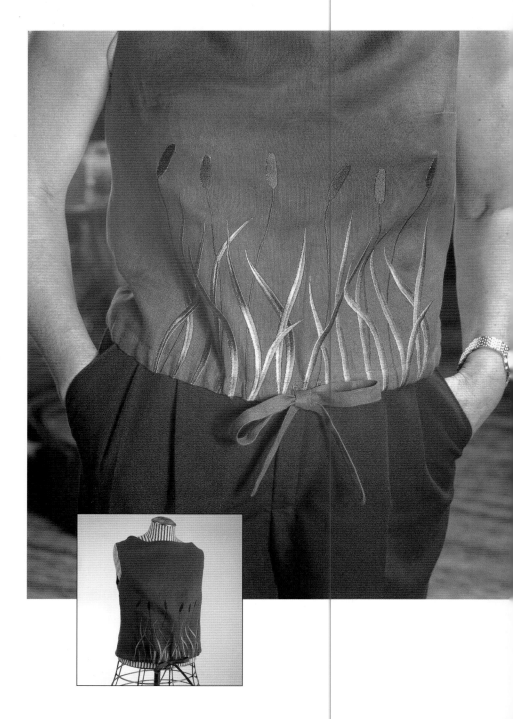

Sewing Supplies

Pattern of choice

Fabric – yardage according to
   pattern

40 wt. rayon thread

Bobbin thread

Tear-away stabilizer

Chalk or water-soluble
   marking pen

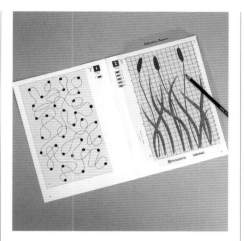

design 3:2 from embroidery card #108 on the Husqvarna Viking Designer 1, or you can select a similar design for your machine.)

1 Lightly trace the front pattern section onto the fabric. Cut around the traced pattern leaving enough fabric along the edges to hoop.

2 Trace the design to the template. (NOTE: Anna used

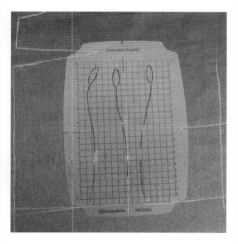

3 Position the template along the bottom edge of the front pattern piece.

4 Layer the fabric over tear-away stabilizer and place in the hoop. Stitch the design following the

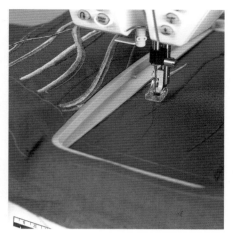

instructions on the machine's screen.

5 Embroider the design twice across the front of the blouse to make a wider embroidery, if desired.

6 Remove the stabilizer and press the design from the wrong side. Place your blouse pattern back on the fabric to check the shape. Cut out the pieces and finish the blouse according to the pattern instructions.

Embroidery Equipment Used

Husqvarna Viking Embroidery
   card #108, design 3:2

Husqvarna Viking Designer 1,
   #1+, and Rose

FAR EAST FLAVOR

Jeanne Harrison, United States

*"The abundance of Far East-
inspired fabrics available
today gave me the impetus
for designing this garment. I
combined the embroidery
designs with traditional
sashiko stitching, as well as
piecing techniques to create
an original outfit."*

Sewing Supplies

Pattern of choice (e.g. Kwik Sew
  #2673)

Coordinating prints of fabric –
  yardage according to pattern
  (Colors I and II)

Solid-color fabric – yardage
  according to pattern plus ½ yard
  (Colors II and IV)

Interfacing according to pattern

1 yard of water-soluble or tear-away
  stabilizer

2 yards of gold metallic soutache braid

40 wt. rayon and gold metallic threads

Bobbin thread

Chalk marker

Quilt basting spray

Permanent marker

Open toe embroidery foot

Candlewicking foot

I Following the pattern instructions, cut out all pieces for Colors I and III. Cut out pattern pieces for Color II adding ½″ all around on the lower skirt and sleeve extension pieces for shrinkage from the embroidery. Cut the front and back pattern extensions 12″ x the length of the pattern piece plus 8″.

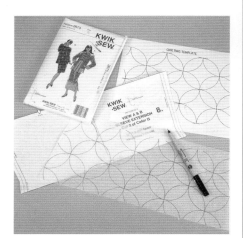

2 To transfer the sashiko stitching lines to the fabric, using the quilting template given here, cut a piece of water-soluble or tear-away stabilizer slightly larger than the pattern pieces for the sleeve extensions and the lower skirt. Trace the stitching lines from the template onto the stabilizer with a permanent marker.

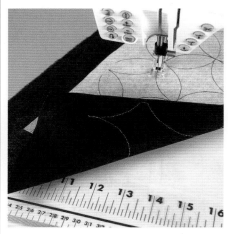

3 Using the basting spray, attach the stabilizer to the wrong side of each sleeve extension and lower skirt sections. Thread your machine with the bobbin thread and place the gold metallic thread on your bobbin. Using a longer-length straight stitch, stitch in a continuous line following the arrows on the stabilizer. Once the stitching is completed, carefully remove the stabilizer. (Using the needle-down feature on your machine helps when pivoting.)

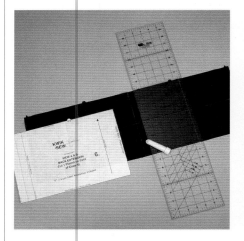

4 To embroider the front and back extensions, place a piece of tear-away stabilizer under the fabric and hoop both layers into the largest hoop. To center the designs on the back extension, draw a chalk line down the center and again at the quarter sections. Also mark the width in half horizontally from end to end. The top of the hoop should be toward the seam line for correct orientation.

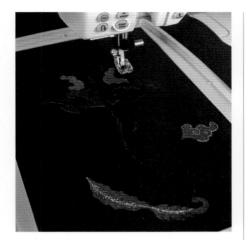  

5 Begin embroidering the design following the instructions given on the screen of your machine. Change thread colors as desired. (Jeanne selected design 1:4 but you can use any design of choice depending on the "flavor" of your garment.)

6 You can change the look of many embroidery designs by stopping in the middle of the stitching of a particular thread color and changing to another color. Veins and some outline stitching was done in gold thread on this design in this manner.

7 Additional thread embellishment can be added to the embroidery designs. Candlewicking stitches give the appearance of small gold beads added to the design. Or select a decorative stitch of your choice on your machine.

8 Check your pattern pieces against the embroidered sections, trimming the fabric as necessary.

 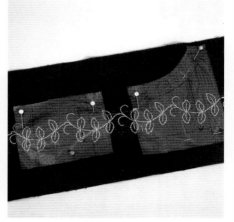 

9 Cut a 5"-wide strip from the Color II fabric. Mark the center with the chalk marker and place a strip of tear-away stabilizer underneath. Thread your machine with the gold metallic thread and place the bobbin thread in the bobbin. Following the marked line, stitch a wide decorative stitch down the center of the strip. (Jeanne used a Husqvarna Viking Omnimotion stitch – K6.)

10 Carefully remove the stabilizer. Cut the neckline patch and front patch from the embroidered strip, centering the design under the templates.

11 Continue completing the jacket according to the pattern instructions through step 7.

12 Add an embellished soutache braid trim between the front inset and the front sections. Using your candlewicking foot and programmed stitch, stitch down the length of the soutache. Finish the jacket and skirt according to the pattern instructions.

Embroidery Equipment Used

Husqvarna Viking Embroidery
    card #109, design 1:4
Husqvarna Viking Designer 1,
    #1+, and Rose

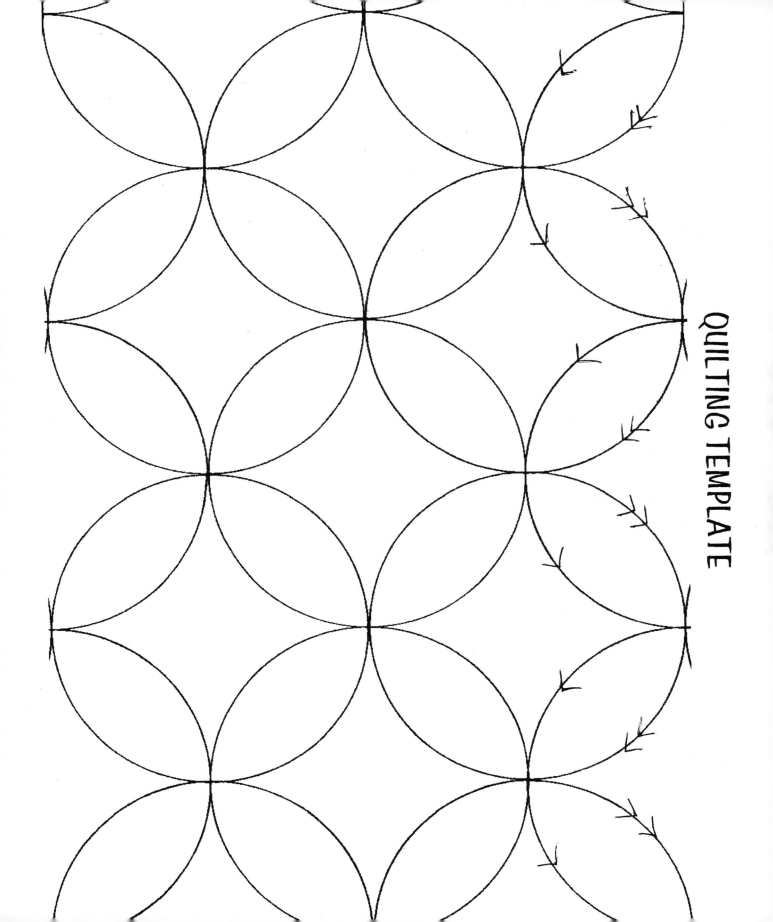

QUILTING TEMPLATE

A TOUCH OF THE ORIENT
FIREPLACE SCREEN

Jeanne Harrison, United States

Sewing Supplies

$7/8$ yard of oriental print cotton fabric

$5/8$ yard dark solid-color fabric

$2¼$ yards of coordinating mottled print

$2½$ yards of heavy cut-away stabilizer or heavy sew-in interfacing

1 piece of 10" x 44" medium-loft batting

1 piece of 12" x 15" medium-loft batting

$7¼$ yards of gold metallic piping

40 wt. rayon and metallic threads

Bobbin thread

Heavy metallic serger thread

Air- or water-soluble marking pen

Chalk marker

40" long - 1" x 4" board

1 - ½" x 19" dowel rod

Large metal snaps

Hooks and eyes

Black indelible marker

Quilt basting spray

Seam sealant

Piping foot

Narrow braiding foot

Pinking shears

Doll hand-sewing needle

stitch the piping to the edge of one mottled strip and one embroidered band. Press the seam toward the mottled strip. Stitch the piping to the other edge in the same manner and repeat on the second embroidered band.

I Cut two strips of solid-color fabric, 5" x 44". Draw a line through the center down the length of each strip with the chalk marker. Back each strip with heavy stabilizer and thread your machine with gold metallic thread and place the bobbin thread in the bobbin. Stitch a wide decorative stitch on each strip using the chalk line as your guide. (Jeanne used an Omnimotion stitch - K5 on her Husqvarna Viking Designer 1.)

2 Cut four strips of the mottled fabric, 2" x 44", and four pieces of the gold piping the same length. With right sides together,

3 Using a dark-color thread, over-stitch all the piping with a zig zag – straight stitch combination. The straight stitches should be toward the solid-color band and the zig zag stitches

should go over the piping, ensuring that the seam will lie flat.

4 For the top band of the fan, cut two strips from the oriental print, 3½″ x 44″. Stitch the print to the embroidered sections placing piping between as in steps 2 and 3.

5 Cut two large pieces from the oriental fabric, 13½″ x 44″. With right sides together, stitch these rectangles to the bottom edge of each stripped/piped section using a ½″ seam allowance with piping between. Follow steps 2 and 3.

6 To mark the fan pleats, draw a line with the chalk marker starting 2″ from a side edge the length of the fan. Continue drawing ten additional parallel lines 3½″ apart across the fan front. Draw the last line 2″ from the previous line. Trim along the last marked line.

7 Using the narrow braiding foot, couch heavy metallic serger thread down the front of the fan sections along the chalk lines with a narrow zig zag.

8 Stitch the heavy stabilizer or interfacing together with a bridging stitch to get two finished pieces, 42½″ x 39″.

9 Cut the fan backing from the mottled fabric the same size as the fan and stiffening sections. On a flat surface, with wrong side up, layer the stiffening material over the backing material. Place the fan front on top, with right side up, and pin all layers together.

10 With a chalk marker, draw a line 2" above the top row of piping. Select a wide, scallop edge-stitch and following the drawn line, stitch with a dark rayon thread in the needle and on the bobbin. After the stitching is completed, outline the thread edge with seam sealant. Once dry, trim the fabric close to the edge.

11 Overcast all the remaining raw edges on both fan sections on your sewing machine or serger.

12 To pleat the fan, fold along the couched thread lines. Edge-stitch close to the fold through all layers.

13 With right sides together, lining up all the bands and piping, stitch the two fan sections together with ¼″ seam allowance.

14 Cut a piece of solid-color fabric, 10″ x 14″; stabilize the piece and place into the large embroidery hoop. (Jeanne selected design 2:4 on her Husqvarna Viking embroidery card #109, which is also an appliqué embroidery design. Or, choose a design for your machine

that is appropriate.) Follow the instructions on the machine screen for starting and stopping and changing thread colors.

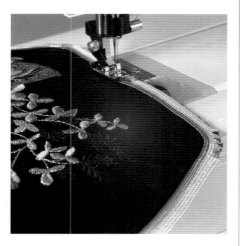

15 Using the Pattern #1 given here, center the design and cut out the section for the fan front. Stitch gold piping to the edge of the embroidered piece. Clip the seam allowance and press to the wrong side.

16 Cut two pieces from the mottled fabric using Pattern #2. Center the piped embroidered piece on the right side of the newly cut mottled piece. Stitch around the piping using the same stitch as you did in step 3. Add piping to the outer edge of this new piece.

17 Pin the remaining pattern piece with right sides together to the piped piece. Layer the pinned section over the smaller piece of batting and, leaving a 2″ opening along the bottom for turning, stitch around all sides. Trim your seams close to the stitching with pinking shears. Turn and press. Fold in open edge and using the stitch in step 3, close the bottom and stitch around entire edge.

PATTERN #1

Cut 1 from Black Fabric

FIREPLACE FAN
Designed by Joanne Harrison

PLACE ON FOLD

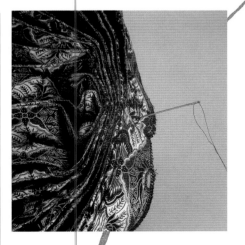

18 Cut a piece of backing fabric 4″ x 19″. Turn in ¼″ twice and stitch in place. Fold the fabric in half lengthwise, wrong sides together; stitch a ¼″ seam. Turn the tube right side out. Press the seam to one side and pin to the fan back seam ½″ from the top edge. Sew the tube to the seam.

19 Thread long, hand needle with a heavy thread. With the fan laid out on a flat surface, form the pleats by folding back and forth along the couched lines. Bring the edges together and hand-tack through all the layers at the center seam line.

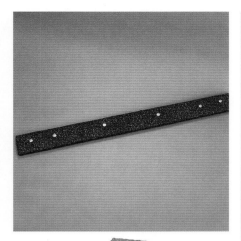

20 Mark the board in the center and 2½″ from one side. Drill a ½″ hole at this marked point. Cut a strip of mottled fabric 10″ x 44″. Place the fabric strip, wrong side up, on a flat surface. Layer the remaining batting piece on top and center the board on top. Wrap the fabric around the board and staple securely in place. Cut an "X" through the fabric and batting over the drilled hole.

21 Insert the dowel rod in the tube and place the end into the hole on the fan base. Pin the embroidered piece to the front of the pleats with the bottom edge against the fan base. Attach hooks and eyes to secure in place. Add heavy-duty snaps to the bottom edges of the fan and screw snap sockets to the fabric-covered base.

Embroidery Equipment Used

Husqvarna Viking Embroidery
   card #109, design 2:4
Husqvarna Viking Designer 1,
   #1+, and Rose

FIREPLACE FAN
Designed by Jeanne Thomason

PATTERN #2

Cut 2 from Red Fabric

PLACE ON FOLD

SEASIDE
BATHROOM

Patrick Lose, United States —

designed by Pamela Hastings

SHOWER CURTAIN

Sewing Supplies

5 yards decorator fabric

1 yard contrasting fabric

    for trim

40 wt. rayon thread

Bobbin thread

Tear-away stabilizer

1 Cut 2 pieces of fabric for the shower curtain, 70″ x the width of the fabric. Sew the shower curtain panels together using a French seam. To create a French seam,

place fabric wrong sides together and stitch with a ¼″ seam allowance. Turn fabric right sides together and stitch again with a ½″ seam allowance.

2 Cut 2 contrasting bands, one 7″ x 70″, and the second, 7″ x the seam width of the shower curtain.

Turn under ½″ along one long edge of each band and press.

3 Mark a 45-degree angle at the end of one band piece. Stitch the band pieces, right sides together, along the marked line. Trim the seam to ¼″ and press open.

4 Pin the seamed band matching the raw edges to the right and bottom edge of the shower curtain, with the right side of the

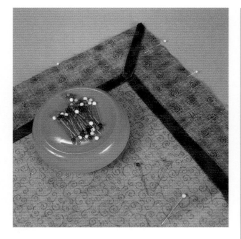

band to the wrong side of the shower curtain. Stitch with a ½" seam allowance.

6 Using the embroidery template, mark the desired location of each fish and embroider. Stabilize the fabric; hoop, and stitch.

8 Turn under and press a 1" double-fold hem on the left-hand edge of the shower curtain. Stitch close to the fold.

9 Turn under a 1½" double-fold hem along the top of the shower curtain and stitch. Mark the placement of the buttonholes along the upper hem approximately 6" apart. Stitch each buttonhole.

5 Turn the band to the right side of the shower curtain and press. Pin the band in place and topstitch close to the fold.

7 Add small buttons near the fish as bubbles for embellishment.

SHOWER CURTAIN VALANCE

1 Cut five triangles, 15″ x 16″ x 16″, from one fabric and five triangles of the same size from the other. Stitch a sample of the desired embroidery on a scrap of

fabric, eliminating any thread changes if desired. Trace the motif onto your template and mark the position on three triangles of one fabric and on two of the other. Stabilize and stitch the motifs.

2 Place one embroidered triangle and one contrasting fabric triangle, right sides together, and stitch around all sides with a ½″ seam allowance, leaving an

opening for turning. Trim the seams and clip the corners.

3 Turn the triangles to the right side and press. Slipstitch the opening closed.

VANITY SKIRT

4 Mark the placement for four grommets along the narrower edge of each triangle, placing one in each corner and two evenly spaced between. Insert the grommets using a grommet tool.

Decorator fabric – yardage according to measurements

Contrasting fabric for band – yardage according to measurements

Tear-away stabilizer

40 wt. rayon thread

Bobbin thread

Velcro™ Half & Half hook and loop tape

I Measure around the front and sides of the vanity. Divide this measurement by 2 and add 1″. Cut two skirt pieces using this measurement x the height of the vanity plus 1″. Cut two bands of contrasting fabric, 4″ x the width of the skirt panels. Cut one band, 4″ x the length of the skirt panel.

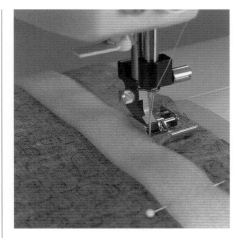

2 Cut two strips of hook and loop tape the width of the skirt minus 1″. Sew one side of the tape to the wrong side of the skirt 1″ from the top edge.

3 Press under ½″ on one long edge of the band piece for the top edge of the skirt.

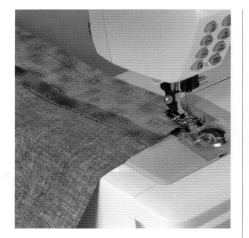

4 Pin the band to the top edge of the skirt, the right side of the band to the wrong side of the skirt. Press the seam open.

5 Fold the band to the right side of the skirt and press. Pin band in place and topstitch along the fold. Prepare and attach remaining bands in the same manner as the shower curtain.

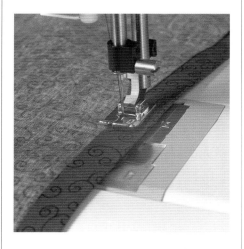

6 Turn under and stitch a ½″ double-fold hem on the outside edges of the skirt.

7 Select your seaside embroideries as desired. Stabilize the fabric and place in the hoop. Stitch your motifs.

BANDED TOWELS

Bath or hand towels –
colors as desired

½ yard decorator fabric

40 wt. rayon thread

Bobbin thread

Water-soluble stabilizer

50mm bias-tape maker

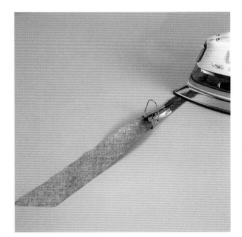

1 Cut 2″ bias strips from decorator fabric. Using a bias-tape maker, press in the edges. The strips should be as wide as the towels plus 1″.

2 Pin the bias strips to the towel front over the woven band.

3 Edge-stitch each band in place along both edges, turning in each end ½″.

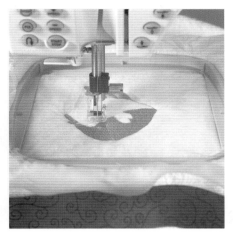

4 Using your embroidery template, center the selected embroidery design above the stitched bias band on each towel. Place the water-soluble stabilizer over the toweling for stitching. Hoop and stitch, changing colors according to the instructions on your machine screen.

Embroidery Equipment Used

Husqvarna Viking Embroidery
card #35, designs 1, 2, 3, 4, 5,
6, and 24

Husqvarna Viking Designer 1,
#1+, and Rose

HANG IT UP

Mary Mulari, United States

"Place this handy, bright spring/summer wall hanging next to your door for your sunglasses, keys, and necessary sunblock!"

Sewing Supplies

1 yard of cotton fabric for backing front and back

¼ yard of solid-color cotton fabric for pockets

¼ yard of 5 different cotton prints for squares and appliqués

40 wt. rayon thread

Bobbin thread

Tear-away stabilizer

Spray adhesive

Thin cotton quilt batting

Fusible web

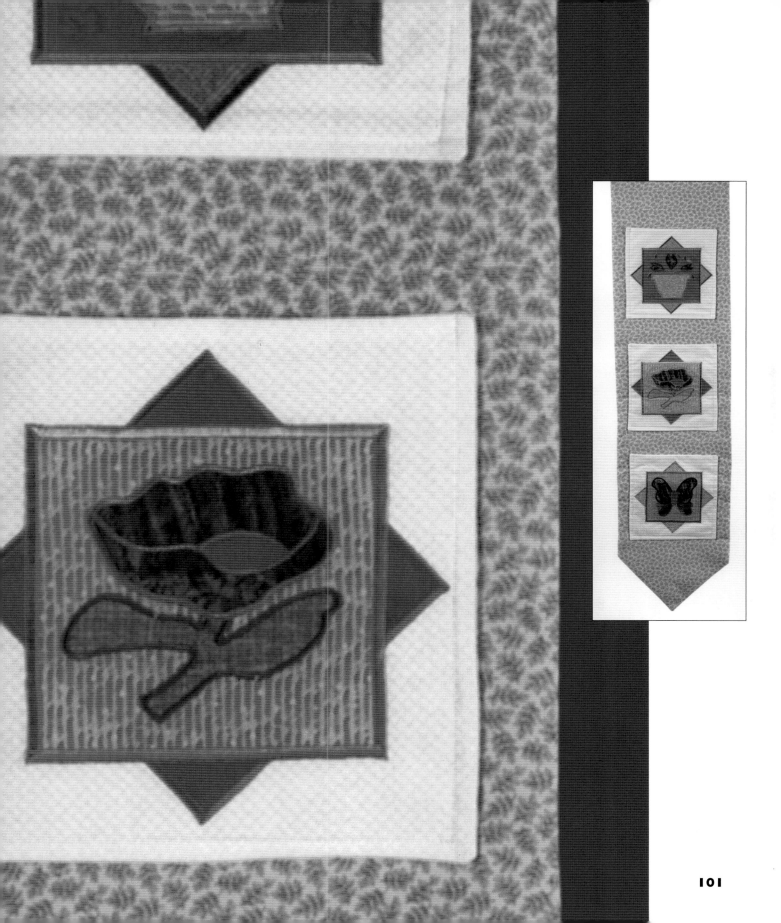

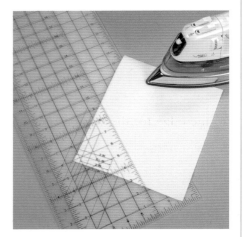

1 Press paper-backed fusible web to the appliqué fabrics.

2 Cut three 15″ x 8″ rectangles for pockets. Fold each piece in half lengthwise with wrong side together and press a crease.

3 Cut six 4½″ squares from the previously fused fabrics. Open out each pocket piece and fuse one square on point ¾″ from the edges with the fold of the pocket

at the top. Fuse the remaining three squares over the other squares centered on the pocket pieces.

4 Select your appliqué embroidery design; stabilize and hoop the pockets, centering appropriately. (Mary chose designs 2, 3, and 6 from Husqvarna Viking card #27.) Following the instructions on your sewing machine screen, layer the first fabric for the embroidery and outline stitch.

5 Without removing the pocket fabric from the hoop, trim the excess fabric away and continue according to the instructions on your machine. (These embroidery designs incorporate multiple layers of appliqué fabrics that are layered and trimmed prior to any satin stitching.)

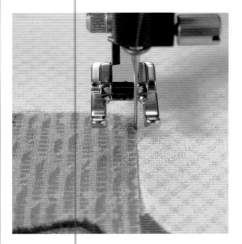

6 As the final step on each pocket, satin-stitch around the edges of the fused squares. Miter the satin stitching at the corners. (On the Husqvarna Viking Designer 1, choose stitch C-14, SL-0.3; SW-5.0; and elongate 2.)

7 With right sides together, stitch each pocket leaving a 1½" opening at the bottom edge for turning. Trim the corners, turn. Press and slipstitch the opening closed.

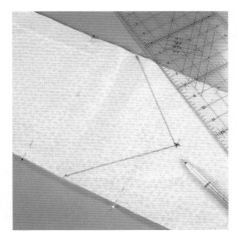

8 Measure and cut out two pieces 38" x 10". Find the center and mark along one end. Measure up 5" along each end. Draw lines from the edge marks to the center mark.

9 Measure down 9" from the top edge and center the first pocket. Topstitch in place on three sides. Space the remaining pockets 2" apart and topstitch in place.

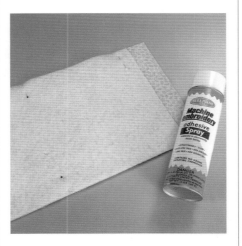

10 Spray the thin cotton batting with the spray adhesive. Allowing 3" at the top for the casing, adhere the batting to the front section and trim the point.

11 With right sides together, stitch the sides and bottom edges. Trim all corners and turn. Press.

12 Turn in ¼" to the inside on the top edge and press. Turn down the top 1½" and stitch close to the edge for the casing. Hang, using a narrow dowel and cord. Add buttons, a tassel, or other forms of embellishment to your wall hanging.

Embroidery Equipment Used

Husqvarna Viking Embroidery
  card #27, designs 2, 3, and 6
Husqvarna Viking Designer 1,
  #1+, and Rose

FLEECY JACKET

Mary Mulari, United States

"Comfy clothing for cold winter days!"

Sewing Supplies

Pattern of choice (e.g. Burda 2860)

Fleece fabric – yardage according to
   pattern

Cotton print fabrics for appliqué

40 wt. rayon thread

Bobbin thread

Water-soluble stabilizer

Spray adhesive

Fusible interfacing

Assorted buttons

Monofilament thread

1 Fuse the interfacing to the wrong side of the cotton print fabrics.

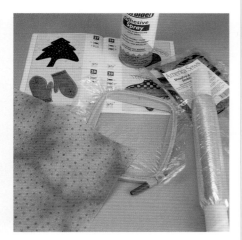

2 The appliqués were created on the stabilizer first before being stitched to the jacket sleeves and hood. Place two layers of the water-soluble stabilizer in the small hoop. Using a spray adhesive, adhere a 4″ square of interfaced fabric onto the hooped stabilizer.

3 Select an embroidery design for your machine. Once the machine has sewn the outline straight stitch, stop and, without removing the stabilizer from the hoop, trim away the excess fabric from the

outer edge. (Mary selected from Husqvarna Viking card #27, designs 21, 26, 27, 28, and 31.)

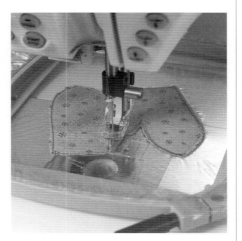

4 Only one-color thread was used to satin-stitch these embroidery designs to create the appliqués. Carefully remove the stabilizer from the back of the appliqué piece.

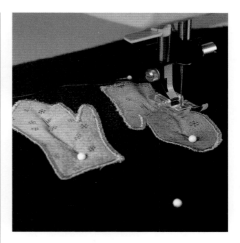

5 Using the monofilament thread on top and a polyester thread on the bobbin, stitch the appliqué pieces to the flat jacket sleeves and hood with a narrow zig zag (W-2, L-2) over the satin stitch.

6 Complete your jacket according to the pattern instructions. This method of appliqué allows you to appliqué fabrics that may pucker or are difficult to satin-stitch directly.

Embroidery Equipment Used

Husqvarna Viking Embroidery
    card #27, designs 21, 26, 27,
    28, and 31
Husqvarna Viking Designer 1,
    #1+, and Rose

SUBTLE GREEN LEAVES

Lill Nylen, Sweden

" I am both inspired by the style of the garment and the fabric that I am going to use when I design my embroideries. The design has to blend well and harmonize with the total look. Of course, the design can just as well be used for other purposes. Choose the design you are going to use with care, so it works with the style and look of your garment.

If you are fortunate enough to own a good sewing machine, you can choose to make your garments out of high-quality fabric and follow the latest trends without spending a fortune. And if your machine also embroiders, you can really personalize your garments and wear something that will be admired by everyone."

Sewing Supplies

Pattern of choice with few seams on the body

Fabric – yardage according to pattern

40 wt. rayon thread

Bobbin thread

Tear-away stabilizer

Chalk or water-soluble marking pen

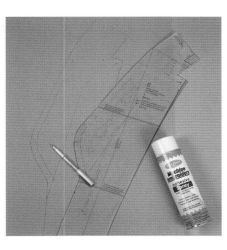

1 Lightly trace the collar pattern piece that will be embroidered onto the fabric. Transfer all markings to the fabric. Cut around the traced pattern leaving enough fabric along the edges to hoop.

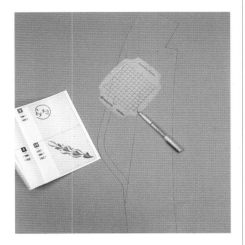

2 Select your design and trace it onto the plastic template. Position the template on the fabric and mark so the embroidery follows

the curve of the collar as much as possible.

3 Layer the fabric over the tear-away stabilizer and place in the hoop. Stitch the design following the directions in your instruction manual or on the machine screen.

4 Remove the stabilizer and press the design lightly from the wrong side. Cut out the pieces and finish the jacket according to the pattern instructions.

Embroidery Equipment Used

Husqvarna Viking Embroidery
     card #16, design 10
Husqvarna Viking Designer 1,
     #1+, and Rose

LOVELY IN ECRU

Lill Nylen, Sweden

"When I design embroideries, I am very selfish and think of myself. I design the type of embroideries that I would want to use myself. As I am a fashion sewer, most of the time it results in designs that I can use on my own garments . Fortunately, I have learned that my designs are also appreciated by other sewers, particularly those who sew fashion garments."

Sewing Supplies

Pattern of choice with few seams

Fabric — yardage according to

    pattern

40 wt. rayon thread

Bobbin thread

Tear-away stabilizer

Chalk or water-soluble marking pen

1 Lightly trace the front and back pattern pieces that will be embroidered onto the fabric, transferring all seam lines and pocket placements. Cut around the traced pattern leaving enough fabric along the edges to hoop.

2 Stitch and press all darts or seams, as necessary, that will be under any embroidery.

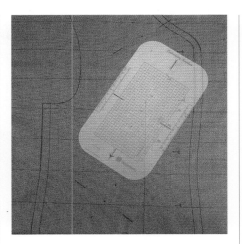

3 Trace the design to the template and mark the positioning on the front and back pieces.

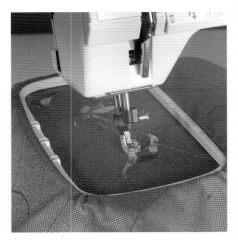

4 Layer the fabric over the tear-away stabilizer and place in the hoop. Stitch the design following the instructions on your sewing machine screen. (Lill used design 17 from Husqvarna Viking card #25, or you can select one appropriate for your machine.)

5 Mark the design placement over the shoulder. Stabilize and hoop the jacket back and mirror-image the design accordingly. Stitch out the design.

6 Remove the stabilizer and press the design from the wrong side. Cut out the pieces and finish the jacket according to the pattern instructions.

Embroidery Equipment Used

Husqvarna Viking Embroidery card #25, design 17

Husqvarna Viking Designer 1, #1+, and Rose

FOR A SPECIAL BABY

Martha Pullen, United States

"Every newborn deserves an elegant heirloom such as this pillow. Passed down through the generations, it becomes even more special."

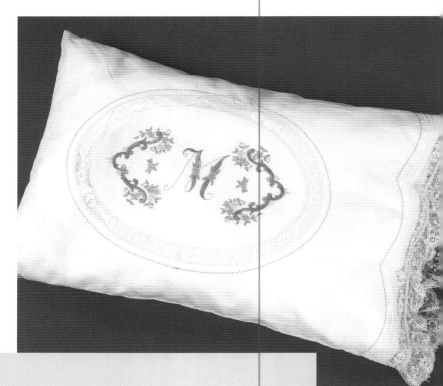

Sewing Supplies

½ yard ecru Swiss batiste, straightened on both ends

1⁷/₈ yards of ³/₄"-wide ecru insertion lace

1²/₃ yards of 1"-wide ecru lace edging

40 wt. rayon thread

Bobbin thread

60 wt. embroidery thread

Lightweight tear-away stabilizer

Lace shaping board

Glass-head straight pins

Press cloth

Air- or water-soluble marking pen

#90 to 110 Universal needle

#1.6/70 double needle

5- or 7-groove pintuck foot

Edge-joining foot

Clear plastic foot

¼" foot

Spray starch

Iron

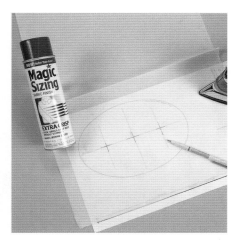

1 Spray-starch the fabric lightly. Remove the selvage from one side of the ½-yard piece of fabric. Measure across the fabric 23½″ and mark. Tear vertically at the mark to create a rectangle of fabric 23½″ horizontally by 18″ vertically. Press. Place the side and lower edge of the fabric along the pattern lines. Trace the three crosshairs for the center placement of the three embroideries using a water-soluble marking pen.

2 Hoop the fabric using two layers of tear-away stabilizer. (The use of a Plus Hoop or the large hoop with the Designer 1 will

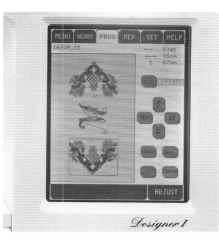

allow all of the embroideries to be completed in one hooping.)

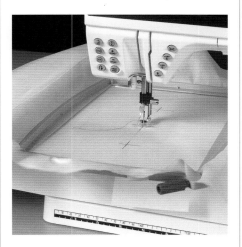

3 Select the desired initial; rotate it so that the bottom of the initial is toward the nearest raw edge. Embroider the initial in the center. Stitch the outer designs on each side.

4 Remove the fabric from the hoop and carefully remove the stabilizer, one layer at a time. Press well.

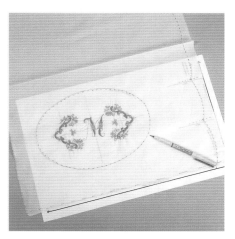

5 Position the embroidered fabric on top of the template. Trace the oval, scallops and miter lines with a water-soluble marking pen. Reposition the fabric and continue tracing the scallops on the back of the pillowcase.

6 Place the fabric on a lace shaping board and pin at each corner. Beginning at the lower center of the oval, shape the lace insertion around the oval, matching the outer heading of the lace to the drawn line. Pin about

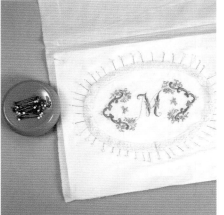

every ¼″, placing the pins in the heading only, almost flat on the fabric with the head of the pins toward the outside of the oval. The inner edge of the lace will be loose and not lay flat on the surface of the fabric. Cut the lace insertion, folding the top edge under ¼″ and overlapping the beginning edge by ¼″.

7 Pull the uppermost thread on the inside edge of the lace

insertion, beginning at the fold on the end that is folded back and at the end of the lace on the other cut end. Gently pull each gathering thread so that the insertion lace lies flat on the fabric.

8 Shape the remaining insertion lace to the scallop line at the lower edge of the pillowcase, placing the lower heading on the marked scallop line. Pin as for the oval. Miter the points by placing a pin in the lace at the top and bottom on the miter lines. Fold the lace back on itself; re-pin the lower pin so that it is through two layers of lace. Continue pinning, matching the lower heading with the drawn scallop line. Gather the upper edge as above.

9 Lightly spray-starch, cover with a press cloth, and press the lace with the tip of the iron. Remove the pins from the heading of the lace and the lace shaping board, and carefully pin the lace to the fabric only.

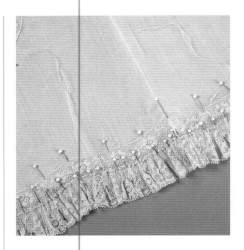

10 Divide the lace edging into fourths by folding twice and mark the quarter points. Mark the quarter points of the open edge of the pillowcase. Gather the lace edging by pulling the uppermost gathering thread of the edging lace. Match the quarter points of the edging to the quarter points of the lace insertion, butting the heading of the lace edging to the lower edge of the lace scallops. Pin well.

11 Insert a large Universal needle and thread with lightweight sewing thread in the needle and bobbin. Attach the edge-joining or a clear foot, and choose the Pin Stitch. (On the Husqvarna Viking Designer 1, it's D-6; L-2.5; W-2.0.) Place one layer of tear-away behind the lace-shaped oval and

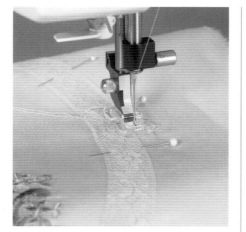

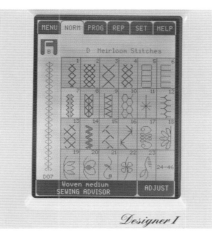

Designer 1

lower edge of the pillowcase under the lace insertion and edging. Stitch the outer edge of the lace oval so that the straight part of the stitch is on the fabric right next to the heading of the lace and the "fingers" of the stitch go into the lace. Repeat for the inner heading of the lace oval remembering to mirror-image the stitch. With the same machine set-up, stitch the lace insertion scallops to the fabric, following the upper edge of the lace.

12 Choose the entredeux stitch and stitch the edging to the insertion, stitching through the fabric of the pillowcase and stabilizer. The center of the stitch should be placed where the laces butt up against each other. (On

the Husqvarna Viking Designer 1, the entredeux stitch is D-7.)

13 Carefully remove stabilizer. Trim the fabric from behind the lace insertion oval, lace insertion scallops, and edging.

14 Place the #1.6/70 double needle in the machine and thread both needles with lightweight sewing thread that matches the fabric. Using the pintuck foot, length of 1.5, position the edge of

the foot next to the stitched lace insertion. Stitch a pintuck above the pin stitch. Repeat again for a second pintuck.

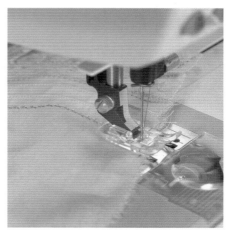

15 Place the tear-away stabilizer on the wrong side above the pintucks and behind the lace oval. Choose the featherstitch (L-2.0; W-2.0) and stitch a row a presser foot's width above the uppermost row of pintucks around the lace

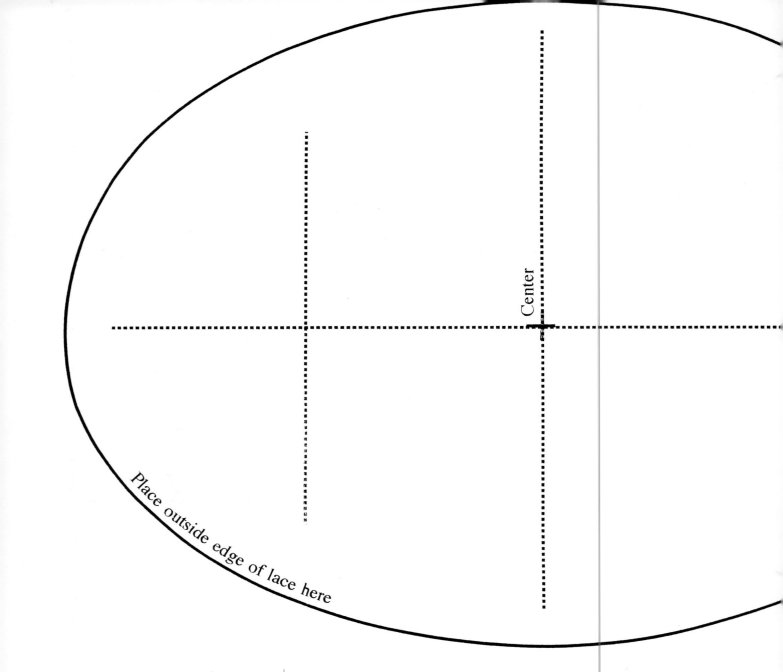

Center

Place outside edge of lace here

oval. Carefully remove the stabilizer.

16 Fold the rectangle in half with right sides together. Stitch across the unfinished end and down the side to the lace edging. The seams can be finished with a zig zag or serger stitch, or use a French seam. Rinse to remove all of the markings and allow to dry. Turn to the right side and press.

Embroidery Equipment Used

Husqvarna Viking Embroidery card #9, designs 33 and letter of choice

Husqvarna Viking Designer 1, #1+, and Rose

Seam line

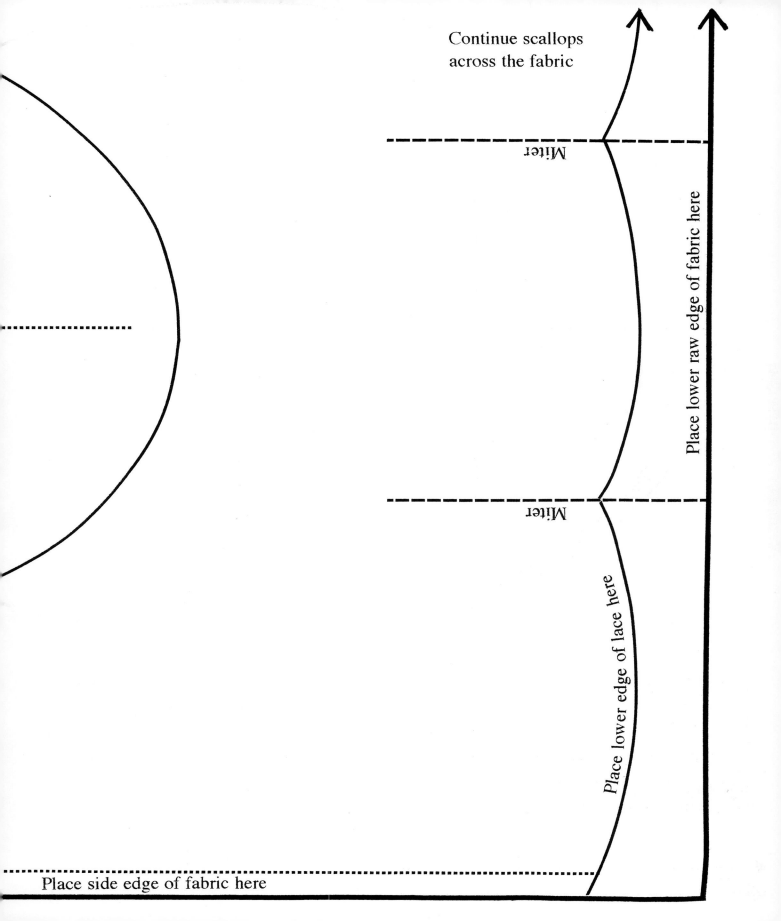

ALL WRAPPED UP

Martha Pullen, United States

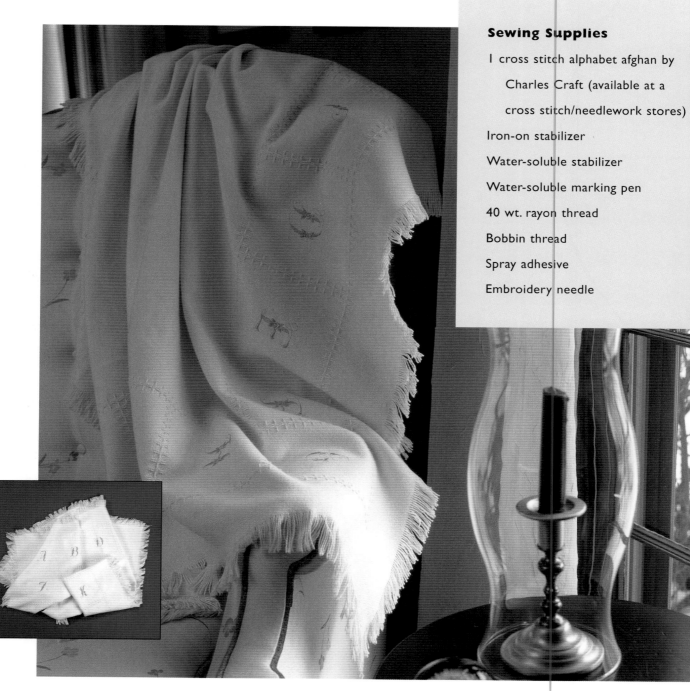

Sewing Supplies

1 cross stitch alphabet afghan by
Charles Craft (available at a
cross stitch/needlework stores)

Iron-on stabilizer

Water-soluble stabilizer

Water-soluble marking pen

40 wt. rayon thread

Bobbin thread

Spray adhesive

Embroidery needle

1 Wash and dry the cotton cross stitch alphabet afghan by Charles Craft.

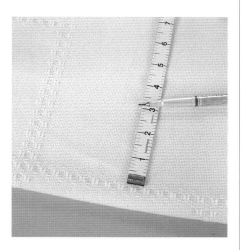

2 Measure each square to determine the center and mark with the water-soluble marking pen.

3 Cut 26 squares or rectangles of iron-on stabilizer (an additional layer of stabilizer may be used for

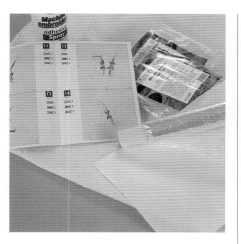

more stability) and water-soluble stabilizer larger than the hoop.

4 Working with one square at a time, iron on the stabilizer to the back of the first square using a medium-hot, dry iron. Spray one side of the water-soluble stabilizer lightly with the temporary spray adhesive and position the sticky side over the center of the square. Hoop the stabilized square and select an "A" from your embroidery alphabet selection.

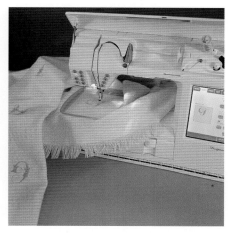

5 Stitch out your design changing colors of thread as necessary. Script or embellished letters will work the best for this project.

6 Continue moving and stitching in each square until the entire alphabet is completed. Remove the stabilizer from each square.

Embroidery Equipment Used
Husqvarna Viking Embroidery
    card #9
Husqvarna Viking Designer 1,
    #1+, and Rose

LIGHT AND AIRY
CURTAIN PANELS

Michelle Pullen, Australia

"It is important that my designs are elegant

but easy for the sewer to achieve."

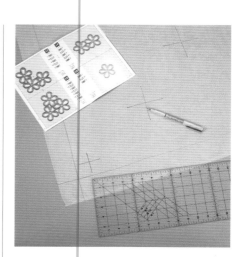

Sewing Supplies

Sheer fabric - yardage

determined by

measurement of

window plus

12" for each panel

40 wt. rayon thread

Spray adhesive

Water-soluble or

tear-away stabilizer

Air-soluble marking pen

Spray seam sealant

Appliqué scissors

1 Determine the length and width of your sheer panels, adding inches at the top for the casings and headers and at the sides and bottom for the hems. Allow extra fabric on all sides for hooping. Softly gathered sheer fabric panels are usually 2-3 times the window width. With an air-soluble marking pen, mark the finished panel dimensions and position the embroideries 18" apart. Use the same rayon thread in the needle and the bobbin for cutwork.

2 Lightly spray two layers of water-soluble or one layer of tear-away stabilizer with the spray adhesive, and position the stabilizer under the first mark. Stitch the first color and once the machine has stitched the second-color outline, remove the hoop

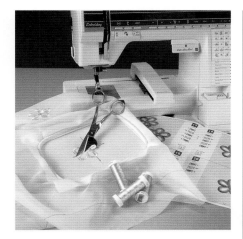

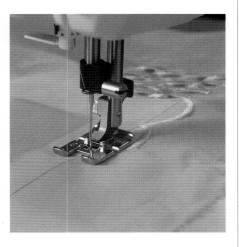

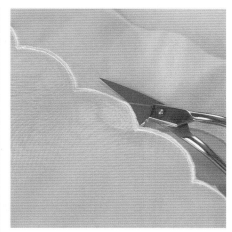

from the machine, and cut the fabric centers away but not the stabilizer. (Embroidery design 20 from Husqvarna Viking card #26 was used. Any comparable cutwork embroidery design can be used.)

3 Finish stitching the second color. Complete the single flower embroideries across all the panels in the same manner.

4 A shaped-corner cutwork design was used on all bottom corners. Follow the same procedure as above for the stitching. (Design 17 chosen was from the Husqvarna Viking card #26.)

5 Cut the tear-away stabilizer into 2″-wide strips. Again, using the spray adhesive, center the stabilizer under the bottom and sides marked hemlines. Select a large satin-stitch scallop and stitch, following the lines.

6 Carefully remove the stabilizer. Lightly spray the back of the scallops with the seam sealant and let it dry. Trim the fabric away close to the scallop stitching and around the embroideries at the

corners with your appliqué scissors.

7 Measure the panels again comparing your measurements. Trim any excess fabric away, allowing 4″ for your header and 2½″ for the casing. Press under ½″ and then 4″ more. Edge-stitch close to edge. Measure up 2″ from stitching line and stitch again, creating the header.

Embroidery Equipment Used
Husqvarna Viking Embroidery
    card #26, designs 17 and 20
Husqvarna Viking Designer 1,
    #1+, and Rose

SPECIAL CUTWORK

Michelle Pullen, Australia

"A little bit of cutwork adds a special touch to towels and a delicate bridal hanky. These little projects make great gifts and you can say "I made them myself."

Sewing Supplies

15" x 18½" linen rectangle for tea towel

30" of velvet ribbon for towel

12½" square of cotton batiste for bridal hanky

25" of satin ribbon for hanky

1½ yards of lace trim for hanky

40 wt. rayon thread

Bobbin thread

Air- or water-soluble marking pen

Water-soluble or tear-away stabilizer

Buttonhole or piping foot

TEA TOWELS

1 Mark up from the bottom edge 2½" for the first ribbon placement. Find the center of this line and mark for the embroidery placement.

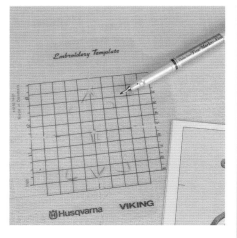

2 Trace the embroidery design onto the template and position using the center mark and the ribbon placement line as guides.

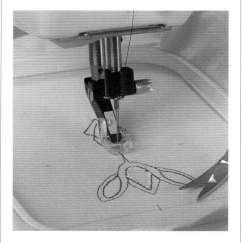

3 Layer your linen rectangle over the stabilizer and hoop. Begin stitching the design, stopping

once the outline stitching is completed. Without removing the fabric from the hoop, trim away the fabric but not the stabilizer. Complete the stitching and carefully remove the stabilizer.

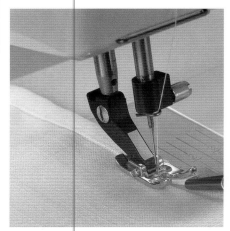

4 Stitch the ribbon along the bottom placement line. Measure and stitch a second row of ribbon evenly spaced above the cutwork design. Using an appropriately sized hemmer foot, hem each edge of the towel.

BRIDAL HANKY

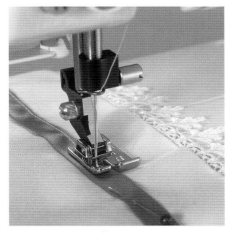

1 Transfer the embroidery design to the template and position in one corner of the batiste square. Mark all guidelines necessary.

2 Stabilize the fabric with either the tear-away or water-soluble stabilizer and hoop. Once the second row of outline stitching has been completed, carefully trim away the inner fabric but not the stabilizer. Continue stitching.

3 Using your buttonhole or piping foot, attach the lace to the edge of the hanky with a rolled hem. Layer the lace trim on the edge with right sides together. Place the raw edge of fabric and

lace under the foot so the right swing of the zig zag will fall off the edge and the left into the fabric. The fabric will roll up over the edge of the lace. Gently curve the lace around the corners.

4 Measure in 1″ from the finished edge and mark for the ribbon placement.

5 Beginning at one corner, stitch the ribbon in place using the marked line. Miter the ribbon at each corner.

Embroidery Equipment Used

Husqvarna Viking Embroidery card #26, designs 21, 24, and 27

Husqvarna Viking Designer 1, #1+, and Rose

AUTUMN LEAVES

Sewing Supplies

Vest and jacket pattern of choice
   (e.g. Simplicity #7985)

1 yard of solid-color 100% cotton

1 yard of print 100% cotton fabric

Tear-away stabilizer

3 or 4 colors of 40 wt. rayon thread

Bobbin thread

Camille Remme, Canada

"A simple vest with fun

details. One special fabric,

such as this lively batik,

adds to the autumn

theme."

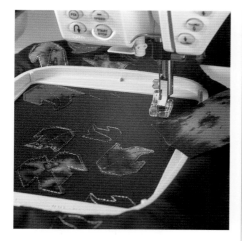

1 Cut the vest and jacket pattern pieces from the appropriate fabrics. All the appliqués will be placed on the solid-color fabric. Stabilize the vest front and place in the hoop. Select your embroidery design, lay a small scrap of print fabric on top, and stitch. (Camille chose designs 11 and 12 from Husqvarna Viking card #14 for her jacket and vest.)

2 Randomly scatter leaves across the vest front and jacket lapels and sleeves. Because this embroidery design is an outline stitch, some leaves were stitched with just thread. Once the stitching is completed, remove the fabric from the hoop and trim away any extra fabric from the top close to the stitching lines.

3 Paper-piece the pocket using the pattern given here from scraps of the print and solid fabrics. Follow the numbers to paper-piece in the correct order. Once completed, cut a 5½″ square for the pocket lining. With right sides together, stitch the lining to the pieced pocket front using a ¼″

seam allowance and leaving a small opening for turning. Remove the paper, trim the corners, and turn. Press and attach pocket to vest front.

4 Complete the vest according to the pattern instructions, lining and binding it with the batik print. Add a fun pin by reducing the size of the piecing pattern and stitching up to, and including, piece #11. Line, turn, and add a clasp to the back.

Embroidery Equipment Used
Husqvarna Viking Embroidery
    card #14, designs 11 and 12
Husqvarna Viking Designer 1,
    #1+, and Rose

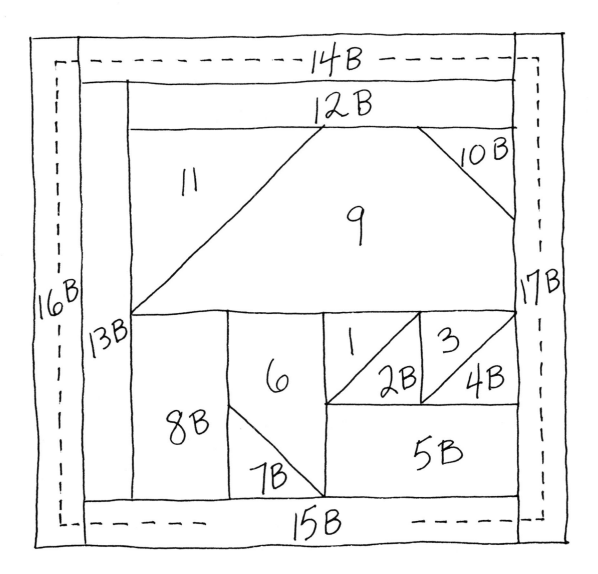

POCKET   -   PAPER PIECE

\#   BLACK FABRIC

\#   PRINT FABRIC

- - - -   STITCHING LINE WHEN POCKET
LINING IS IN PLACE

CELTIC PRIDE

Camille Remme, Canada

"The fun here is that Celtic design is much older in time than Christmas. Both these projects—the placemats and table runner—are reversible and usable all year long."

Sewing Supplies

1 yard of red 100% cotton fabric

1½ yards of black 100% cotton fabric

1 yard of cotton batting

40 wt. rayon thread in red and black

Bobbin thread

Air-soluble marking pen

Rotary cutter, mat, and ruler

PLACEMATS

1 For the placemats, cut two 13″ x 17″ rectangles each from the red and black fabrics and the batting. Sandwich the batting between a red and black piece with right sides of the fabric out; pin. With the red side up, find the center of the layers and mark for embroidery placement.

2 Hoop with the red fabric on top, centering the design using the template. Thread your machine with black thread and place the red thread on the bobbin. Stitch out your design. Stitch again for a bolder look. (Camille selected a design from Husqvarna Viking card #14, or you can choose one appropriate to your machine.)

3 Remove the layers from the hoop and press. Mark in 4″ from each end and topstitch or add a

decorative stitch for extra detail. Trim the placemats to 12″ x 16″.

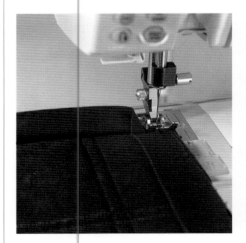

4 Cut a strip, 2″ wide x diameter, of black fabric for binding. Fold in half and press. Matching raw edges, stitch the folded strip to the edges, mitering the corners. Fold the strip over the edge and stitch again close to the edge.

TABLE RUNNER

5 To make the Celtic pieced sections for the table runner, cut the following: red—sixteen pieces-1½″ x 2½″; twenty-four pieces-1½″ square; six pieces-1½″ x 9½″; and black—eight pieces-1½″ x 2½″; four pieces-2½″ square; twenty pieces-1½″ square. Join the strips according to the photo here to make two complete knot designs.

6 Cut four 10″ squares of black. Cut each square in half diagonally. Stitch these triangles to each side of the pieced knots. Trim the block to 13½″ x 13½″.

7 From the black fabric, cut four pieces, 1¾″ x 13½″, and one piece, 16½″ x 13½″. Stitch the narrow strips to the top and bottom of each pieced square. Stitch the remaining rectangle between the two pieced sections along a non-banded side. The resulting piece should measure 13½″ x 42½″.

8 Cut one piece, 13½″ x 42½″, from the red fabric and one from the batting. Sandwich the batting between the red piece and the pieced back with right sides out. Pin to avoid any shifting.

9 With black thread in both the needle and on the bobbin, satin-stitch around the Celtic knot, stopping and starting as necessary. (NOTE: The design will be created on the red side making the runner reversible.)

10 Bind the edges of the table runner as you did for the placemats.

Embroidery Equipment Used
Husqvarna Viking Embroidery
   card #14, design 1
Husqvarna Viking Designer 1,
   #1+, and Rose

SCANDINAVIAN RHAPSODY

Inger Westerberg, Sweden

"Scattered embroidered flowers on cotton fabric are perfect for little girls and boys."

Sewing Supplies

Pattern of choice (e.g. jacket and jumpsuit –
New Look #6880; dress Butterick #6227)

Fabric – yardage according to pattern

40 wt. rayon thread

Bobbin thread

Tear-away or adhesive stabilizer

Air- or water-soluble marking pen

Purchased cap

Purchased T-shirt

JUMPSUIT AND JACKET

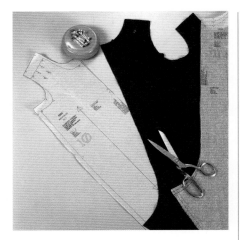

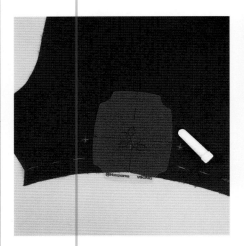

I Cut out the jumpsuit according to the pattern directions and sew the center front and the side seams. Do not sew the crotch seam or center back until the embroidery is completed. Press all the seams open.

2 Trace the embroidery design onto the template and mark one embroidery at the center front of the jumpsuit, with the center of the embroidery 3½" from the finished edge.

3 Stabilize the fabric and hoop. Stitch out your design. (A blueberry motif was used here

from Husqvarna Viking card #22, design 24. Or select a design of your choice for your machine.)

4 Mark the placement for three more embroideries at the lower edge of each leg at the sides. The middle embroidery should be centered on the side seam of the jumpsuit, mark it, and then mark one at each side. The centers of each embroidery should be 5" apart and the finished bottom of the embroidery should be ½" from the finished edge of the jumpsuit. Stabilize and stitch.

5 Sew the center back and crotch seams and finish the jumpsuit according to the pattern directions.

6 Trace the outline of the jacket pattern onto the fabric. Mark the embroidery design randomly on the front of the jacket, leaving 1½"

on all edges without any embroidery. Stabilize and stitch the embroideries.

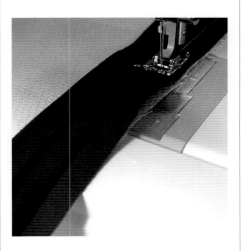

7 Carefully remove all the stabilizer. Assemble the jacket according to the pattern instructions, eliminating the lining. Cut 2" bias strips from the remaining jumpsuit fabric and piece until you have a length to finish the neck, hem, and sleeve edges. Press under ½" along each long side to make 1" bias tape. With the right side of the bias tape to wrong side of the jacket, open out and stitch along the crease of the tape.

8 Fold the bias tape to the right side of the jacket and edge-stitch in place. Finish the center front, neck, and sleeve edges in the same manner.

9 On a purchased T-shirt, mark the embroidery at the center front close to the neck edge. Stabilize and stitch. Repeat the same procedure on the cap.

DRESS AND PINAFORE

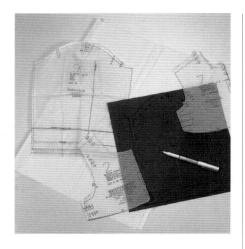

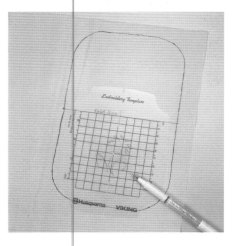

1 Trace all the pattern piece onto the fabric in the appropriate size for both the dress and the pinafore.

2 Draw the design onto the template marking the center starting point. (Designs 15, 17, 19, and 20 were used. Select similar designs for your machine.)

3 Mark the design placement on the pinafore bodice and pockets using the template.

4 Stabilize the fabric and place in the hoop. If the fabric piece is too small for the hoop, use adhesive stabilizer to adhere the fabric to the top. Stitch out your design.

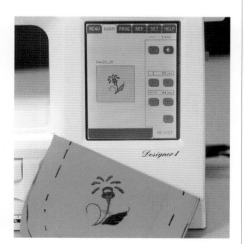

5 Before stitching the second pocket, remember to mirror-image the design.

6 Trace off the designs for the sleeves, bodice, and hem of the dress on the large template.

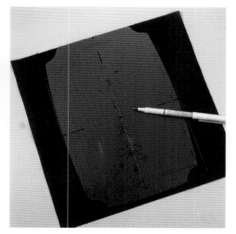

7 Mark the design placement on the fabric indicating the starting points of all designs.

8 Using the largest hoop, line up the combination of designs to be

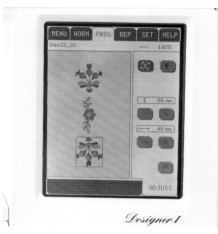

Designer 1

sewn. (With the Customizing feature on the Husqvarna Viking Designer 1, three designs can be stacked and maneuvered before sewing.)

9 Stabilize and stitch out all the designs on the markings. Carefully remove the stabilizer, press, and complete the garments according to the pattern instructions.

Embroidery Equipment Used

Husqvarna Viking Embroidery
   card #22, designs 15, 17, 19,
   20, and 24

Husqvarna Viking Designer 1,
   #1+, and Rose

WARM AND SNUGGLY

Inger Westerberg, Sweden

"Popular fleece fabric is a

perfect medium for embroidery."

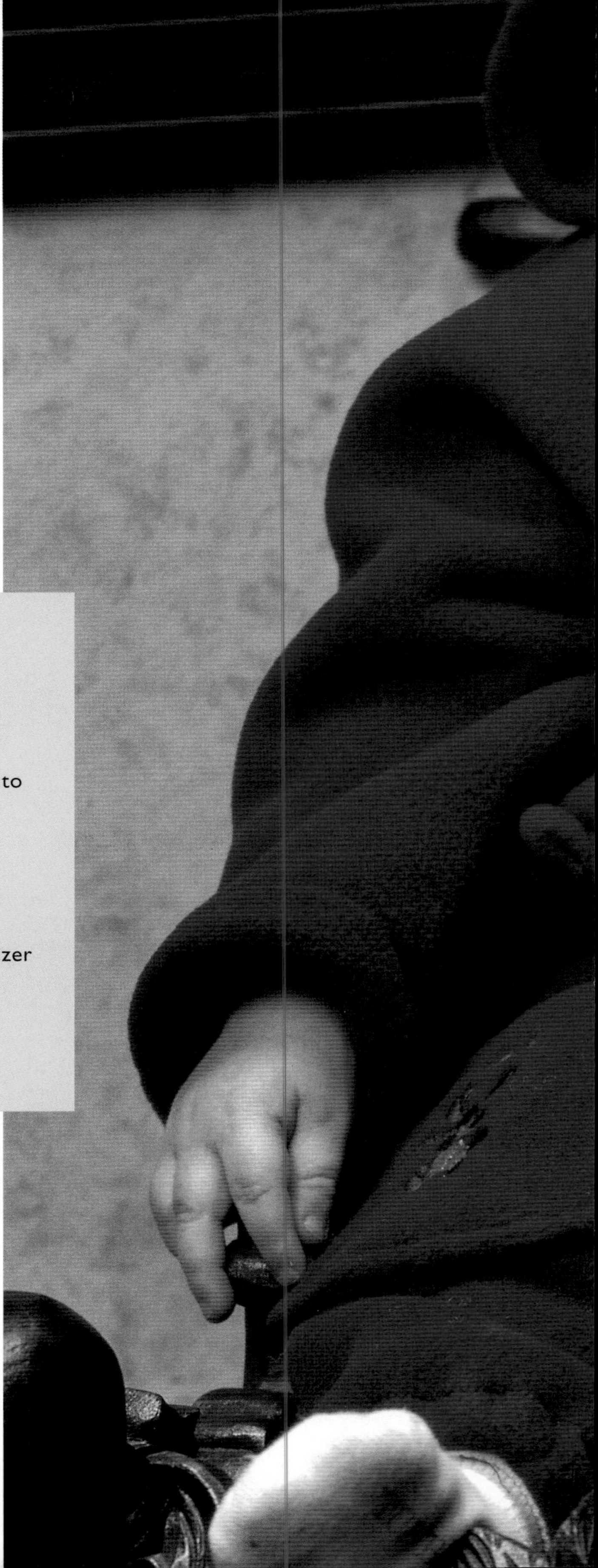

Sewing Supplies

Pattern of choice (e.g. Butterick

#5164)

Fleece fabric – yardage according to

pattern

40 wt. rayon thread

Bobbin thread

Water-soluble and adhesive stabilizer

Rotary cutter, mat, and ruler

Covered button kit

1 Cut out all the pattern pieces for the jacket and the romper. Sew the center and sides together on the romper according to the sewing instructions. Cut two pocket pieces 5″ x 5″.

2 Trace the design onto the template and center onto the pocket pieces. Apply the adhesive stabilizer to the back of the hoop and water-soluble stabilizer on top of the fleece. Place all layers in the hoop.

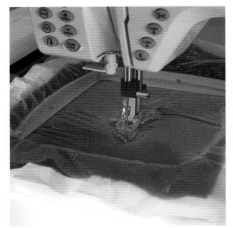

3 Stitch the design changing colors as necessary. (Design 23 from Husqvarna Viking card #22 was used, or you can select a design appropriate to your machine.)

4 Remove the stabilizers from the front and back. Trim the pockets to 3½″ x 4″ once the embroidery is completed.

5 Press in the top edge 1″ and the bottom and sides ½″.

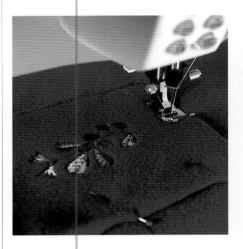

6 Topstitch the pockets to the front of the romper legs centered over the knee area. Complete the romper according to the pattern instructions.

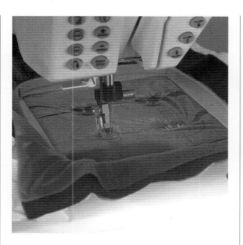

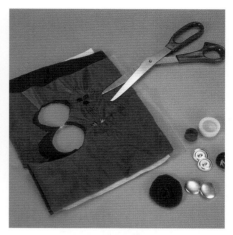

7 Construct the jacket and hood according to the pattern instructions. Add loops and buttons to the jacket front as a decorative detail or use as the closures.

8 Trace the button template onto the water-soluble stabilizer.

9 Layer the adhesive stabilizer under the fleece and the water-soluble stabilizer on top in the hoop. Using only a portion of the design, stitch out the button covers in the colors desired. (Move the starting position on your screen to correspond with the marks on the stabilizer.)

10 Construct the covered buttons according to the manufacturer's instructions.

Embroidery Equipment Used
Husqvarna Viking Embroidery
    card #22, design 23
Husqvarna Viking Designer 1,
    #1+, and Rose

TOP IT OFF

Kerstin Widell, Sweden

*"Allow the pattern to help
dictate the flow of the
embroidery designs. The
gentle curve on the front
panel of this blouse just
begged for an
embellishment!"*

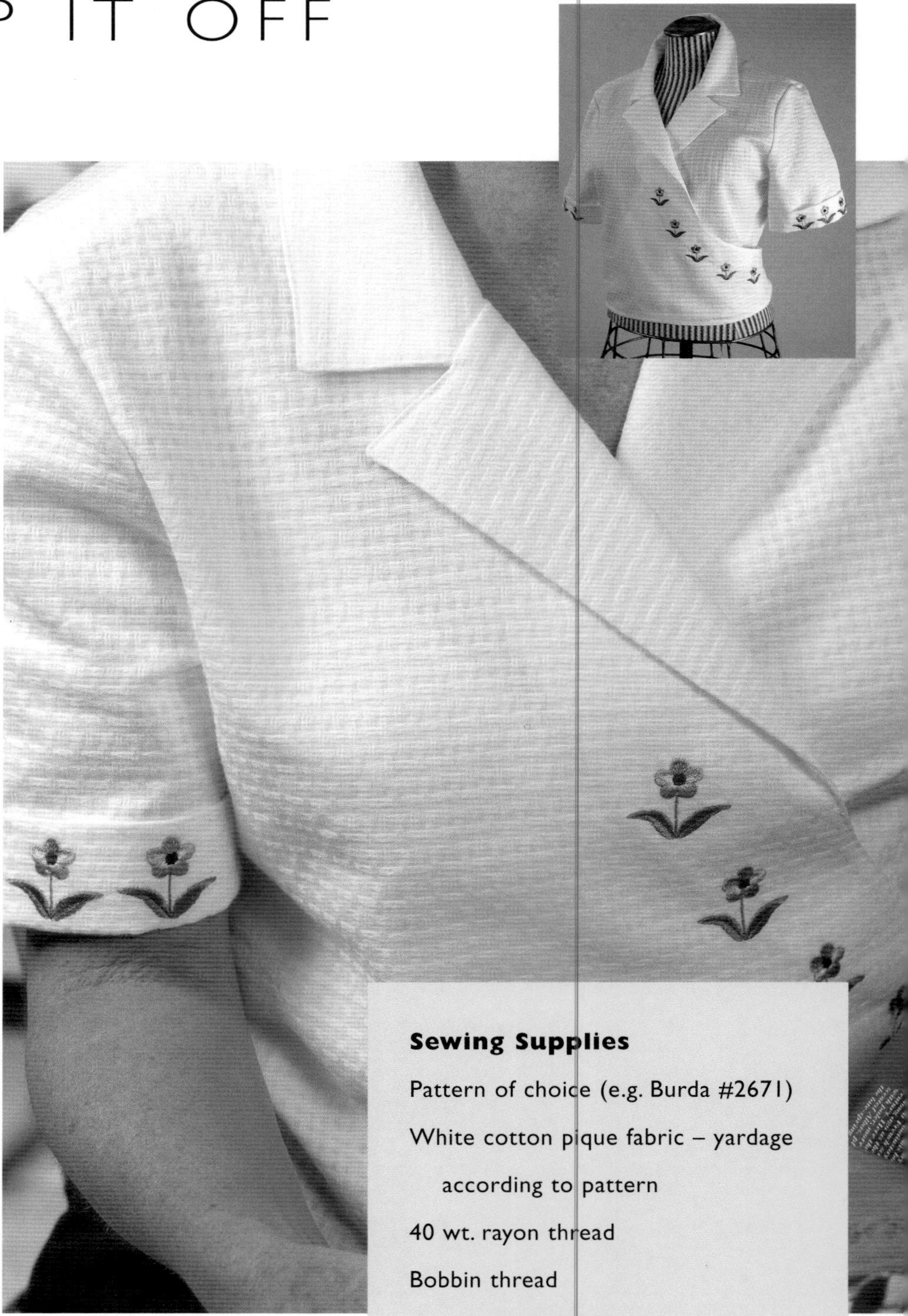

Sewing Supplies

Pattern of choice (e.g. Burda #2671)

White cotton pique fabric – yardage
according to pattern

40 wt. rayon thread

Bobbin thread

Tear-away stabilizer

Air- or water-soluble marking pen

1 Using your air- or water-soluble marking pen, lightly trace the front bodice section onto the fabric. Transfer any important construction markings, such as the collar roll line, to the fabric. Cut out the bodice piece leaving enough fabric to hoop along all edges.

2 Repeat the above procedure on each sleeve section, marking all foldlines for the hems and cuffs.

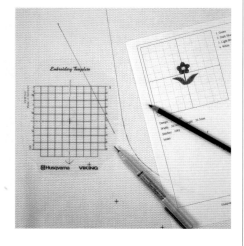

3 Spacing evenly, mark the placement for the five designs on the bodice front using your embroidery template.

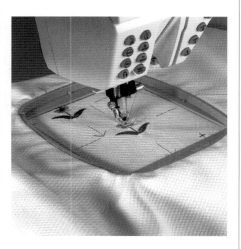

4 Stabilize the fabric and stitch out the flower design down the front, moving the small hoop each times.

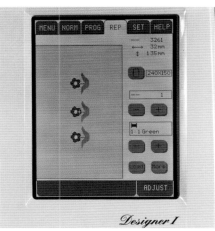

5 Mark each sleeve for the flower design. (Kerstin used the built-in Customizing feature of the Husqvarna Viking Designer 1 to rotate the design and repeat, placing three flowers in a row.)

6 Stabilize your fabric appropriately and stitch out the design on both sleeves. Remove the stabilizer from all the motifs.

7 Check the pattern tissue against the traced lines. Cut out the pieces and continue constructing the blouse according to the pattern instructions.

Embroidery Equipment Used

Husqvarna Viking embroidery
    card #32, design 2

Husqvarna Viking Designer 1,
    #1+, and Rose

SKIRTING AROUND

Kerstin Widell, Sweden

*"This wrap skirt is a
perfect palate for
embroidery. The tone-on-
tone effect is very subtle yet
sophisticated."*

Sewing Supplies

Pattern of choice (e.g. Burda #2735)

Linen or rayon fabric – yardage
according to pattern

40 wt. rayon thread in shade slightly
darker than fabric

Bobbin thread

Tear-away stabilizer

Air- or water-soluble marking pen

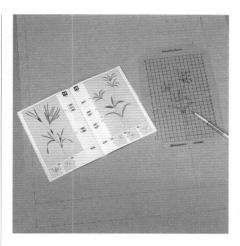

1 This pattern was changed to create a wrap-front skirt. Cut out two front panels, a back panel, a 4"–5" wide left front facing, a waistband, and two ties, one long enough to encircle the waist. With the marking pen, lightly trace the left front panel onto the fabric.

2 Mark the design placement on the fabric using the embroidery template. Four motifs were stitched on the panel. Leaving enough fabric along the edge for

hooping, cut out the left front panel.

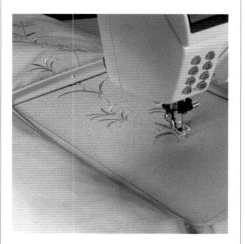

3 Stabilize the fabric as necessary and stitch out the design. (Kerstin was able to use the STOP button on the Husqvarna Viking Designer 1 to delete any color changes as the entire motif was stitched using the same thread color.)

4 Check the sizing of the traced pattern piece against the original before cutting the panel completely out. Stitch the right and left panel pieces to the back section.

5 Fold back the right panel edge ½" twice and stitch forming a hem. Stitch the facing piece to the left front panel edge. Clean-finish any raw edges with your overlock machine.

6 Attach the waistband following traditional sewing techniques, turning and stitching the ties to each end. Sew a buttonhole through the waistband above the right side seam for the tie to go through. Complete by hemming as desired.

Embroidery Equipment Used

Husqvarna Viking Embroidery
    card #36, design 20
Husqvarna Viking Designer 1,
    #1+, and Rose

FLOWERS IN THE GARDEN

Inetta Word, United States

"Use your embroidery

designs for home

decorating items. Combine

many designs to make a

beautifully-framed

picture."

Sewing Supplies

18" x 18" square of linen fabric

Tear-away stabilizer

40 wt. rayon thread

Bobbin thread

Air- or water-soluble marking pen

Tracing paper

Pencil

Compass

Spray starch

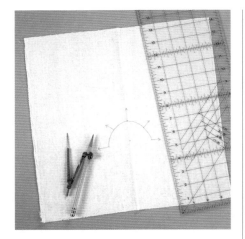

I Starch the 18″ square with spray starch and press. Fold the square in half and press. Measure up the foldline and mark at the 6″ point. Using the mark as the highest point, draw a 3″ half circle as shown. Draw arrows from the circle for leaf placement.

2 Select a large leaf motif and trace onto the template. Position the template around the half circle, marking the starting points for five leaves. Mirror-image the leaves as necessary. Stabilize the fabric and stitch out the leaves, moving the hoop and centering using the marks.

3 Choose a second leaf design and trace onto the template. Place the template on the fabric square and mark the starting points. Stabilize and stitch as before. (Inetta used designs 33 and 34 from Husqvarna Viking card #30

for steps 2 and 3. Choose a design appropriate on your machine.)

4 Continue adding background leaves as desired.

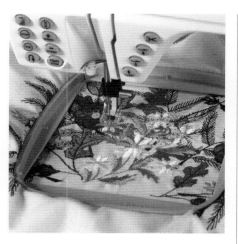

5 You can also stitch out just part of the embroidery design by advancing to the color or section of the design you desire. Remembering to stabilize the fabric, add flowers, buds, and stems, keeping the stitching around the half circle.

6 The stitch length can be adjusted in each embroidery and the starting position can be moved on screen. Adjust your designs as necessary to achieve the effect that you desire.

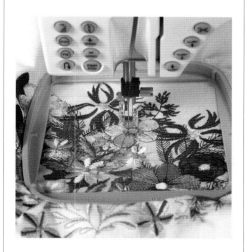

7 Fill in the design with more flowers, adding bright colors across the whole design.

8 Remove the stabilizer once all the stitching is completed. Clip the threads as necessary and press from the wrong side. To preserve your work, professional framing is recommended.

Embroidery Equipment Used

Husqvarna Viking Embroidery
   card #30, designs 2, 3, 4, 9, 10,
   20, 21, 31, 32, 33, and 34
Husqvarna Viking Designer 1,
   #1+, and Rose

AN HEIRLOOM CHRISTENING

Inetta Word, United States

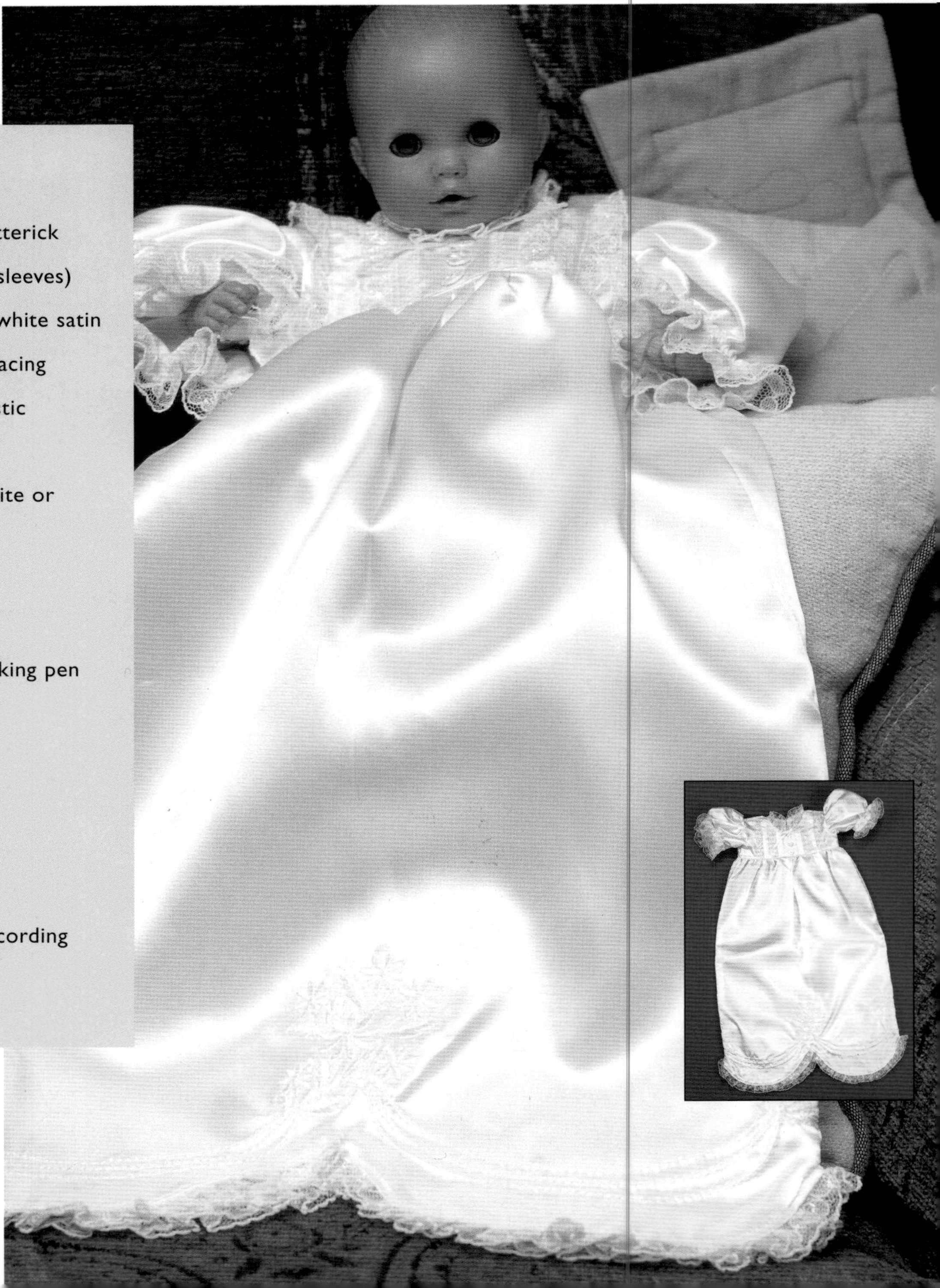

Sewing Supplies

Pattern of choice (e.g. Butterick
   #4588 for bodice and sleeves)

1 ½ yards of white or off-white satin

1 yard fusible nylon interfacing

½ yard of ⅛" braided elastic

5 yards of ½" edging lace

40 wt. rayon thread in white or

   off-white

Bobbin thread

Tear-away stabilizer

Air- or water-soluble marking pen

#2.5 double needle

#100 wing needle

5-groove pintuck foot

Edge-joining foot

Scallop template

Any additional notions according

   to the pattern

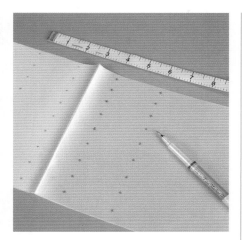

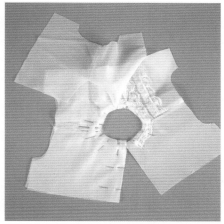

1 Cut a 18″ x 6″ rectangle from the satin. Fold in half lengthwise and press a crease. Using your marking pen, measure 1″ from each side of the fold and mark with dots the width of the strip. Mark a second line 2″ from the first.

2 Select a decorative stitch on your machine and thread the machine with matching rayon thread. (Inetta used stitch N29 on the Husqvarna Viking Designer 1.)

Fold the rectangle along the marked line nearest the fold and stitch the decorative stitch along the edge. Repeat along all lines.

3 After stitching each tuck, stitch a piece of lace under the folded edges with a straight stitch. The edge-joining foot will help guide the fabric here.

4 Place the bodice (yoke) front pattern piece on the tucked fabric and cut out. Also cut the remaining pattern pieces from the satin. Cut front and back bodice (yoke) pieces from the fusible

nylon interfacing. Sew the front and back bodice pieces and the fusible nylon interfacing pieces together at the shoulders.

5 Pin the lace around the neck edge on the satin, pulling the header thread to gather around the curve. With right sides together, lay the interfacing section on the satin piece, matching the neck edge and center back. Sew around the back opening and neck edge using a ¼″ seam allowance. Clip the curves and trim the corners.

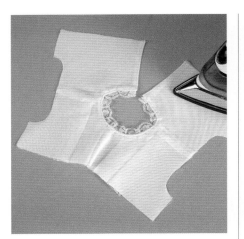

6 Turn the lining to the inside. Press flat being careful not to let the fusible cause wrinkles on the satin. Edge-stitch around the back opening and neckline.

7 Clean finish the bottom edge of each sleeve piece on your serger. Insert the wing needle, thread the machine with the rayon thread, and select a entredeux stitch on your machine. (Inetta used the entredeux stitch, D7, on the Husqvarna Viking Designer 1.)

Lap the lace over the finished edge and attach the lace to the bottom edge of each sleeve.

8 Select a wide zig zag or elastic stitch on your machine. The stitch should be wider than the elastic being attached. Stitch the elastic ½″ above the lace on each sleeve, leaving a small tail at each end. Pull the elastic to the size desired.

9 Sew the front and back skirt, wrong sides together, with a ¼″ seam allowance and make a French seam to avoid any raveling. Leave the center back seam open.

10 Draw a scallop edge along the bottom hem using a scallop template. Trim along the marked line. Pin the lace approximately ¼″ in from the scalloped edge, gathering the lace as necessary and stitch in place. Cut a piece of the fusible nylon interfacing the width of the skirt panel x 5″. With right sides together, stitch the interfacing to the scalloped hem along the lace stitching line. Trim away any excess fabric; notch the curves and turn. Carefully press the fusible interfacing in place.

 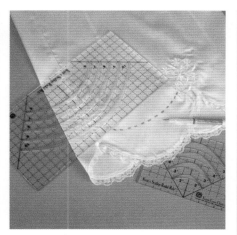 

11 Select an embroidery design for the lower skirt. Stabilize the fabric and hoop. Thread the machine with the rayon thread and using the template center the design over a scallop point. Stitch each design. (Inetta used design 21 from Husqvarna Viking card #30.) Sew the center back seam and stitch a design over the seam.

12 Draw a dotted line with the scallop template between the embroidery designs for pintucks.

13 Using your double needle and 5-groove pintuck foot, stitch along the marked line. Stitch two more rows of pintucks above the first, approximately one presser foot-width apart.

14 Finish the gown according to the pattern instructions.

Embroidery Equipment Used

Husqvarna Viking Embroidery
   card #30, design 21

Husqvarna Viking Designer 1,
   #1+, or Rose

ABOUT THE DESIGNERS

Snez Babic, Canada

Snez Babic is a freelance educator with Husqvarna White Sewing Machines in Canada. For more than 10 years, Snez has shared her knowledge and enthusiasm with sewers across her country. She has made appearances on the PBS television series "America Sews with Sue Hausmann" and is the quilting editor for Husqvarna Viking's international *ZIGZAG magazine*. Snez and her partner, Janice Wray, host the website http://www.thegiftyoumake.com featuring sewing and knitting projects, embroidery designs and an electronic magazine all made with gift-making and -giving in mind.

elinor peace bailey, United States

Born in the Midwest and raised just outside New York City afforded elinor an extraordinary education. Beginning at Parson's School of Design, the Art Students League and Tyler School of Fine Arts at Temple University, she was then led to Brigham Young University to finish her college years and begin graduate work. She and her husband, a musician and teacher, share a unique division of family duties as elinor travels and teaches women to make dolls.

elinor is the creative consultant for *CRAFTS Magazine*; has designed fabric for Concord Fabrics and Daisy Kingdom; has written the books *Mother Plays With Dolls* and *The Rag Doll, From Plain to Fancy*; and has published and marketed her own line of doll patterns and booklets.

A creative force within the doll, crafting, and quilting worlds, elinor's colorful approach to design and life makes her a memorable personality. Her enthusiasm and commitment to doll-making has excited stitchers the world over.

Carola Boberg, Sweden

Carola develops and tests new products, accessories, and embroidery cards in the Development Department at Viking Sewing Machines AB in Sweden. She has studied electro-mechanical engineering, textile technologies and sewing (garment) and has been with Viking since the beginning of 1998.

Work and hobbies sometimes go hand in hand and so it is for Carola. She has been sewing since she started to walk, beginning with sewing clothes for her Barbie dolls and then a few years later sewing clothes for herself.

Terry Fox, Great Britain

Terry Fox is a trained fashion designer, author, and sewing expert. Having been involved in the world of fashion for some 23 years, her background and career are both fascinating and impressive. After qualifying in fashion design, Terry worked for top designers, Zandra Rhodes, Beleville Sassoon, and the Emmanuels. She began to develop her own style and decided to take the plunge with the launch of her own label. Her first collection of evening, wedding, and special occasion wear at Harrods, Knightsbridge, London, was a total sellout!

Having been asked by a well-known department store to lecture on her designs, Terry soon realized her future lay in sharing the inside secrets of the couture world. With the popularity of these lectures soaring, Terry now holds a number of specialized workshops, producing some of the most confident and highest paid dressmakers in the world.

No stranger to television and radio, Terry has been interviewed on a number of programs and has presented an 18-part BBC television series entitled "Wear It Well," covering all aspects of fashion. Her tips and techniques can be found regularly in international magazines and on video. She is the author of *The Terry Fox Fashion Collection*, covering all aspects of couture and professional dressmaking.

Ingrid Larson Haglund, Sweden

An interior designer since 1973, Ingrid Larson Haglund lives with her husband on the island Visingsö, situated in the southern part of Lake Vättern not far from the town of Husqvarna in Sweden. She and her husband own a summer restaurant on the island. Ingrid has also written and illustrated two historical cookbooks about Count Per Brahe who lived in Visingsö more than three hundred years ago.

Anna Haraldsson, Sweden

Designer, Viking Sewing Machines AB, Sweden

Jeanne Harrison, United States

Turning her more than 25 year-old sewing hobby into a money-making proposition enabled Jeanne Harrison to design unique garments while supporting herself and her two children. From there, her self-training in programming and desktop publishing on computers broadened her horizons and gave her the basis for merging her two loves—sewing and computers. As a sewing teacher and computer-digitizing specialist, Jeanne enjoys working with new sewers, sharing her love of sewing and expressing her creativity through her embellished garments.

Patrick Lose, United States

Lose's bright, animated art has graced many a medium in the hobby and craft industry, including a successful line of fabrics from Timeless Treasures. He has spent his professional career in a variety of creative fields, beginning as an actor and singer and costume designer for both stage and screen. His "doodles" are part of the Husqvarna Viking Embroidery collection of works and can be used on quilts, wearable art, home decorating items, and many other craft projects.

His crafts, clothing, and home decorating accessories have appeared frequently in many distinguished magazines including *AMERICAN PATCHWORK, BETTER HOMES & GARDENS, COUNTRY CRAFTS*, and *CREATIVE SEWING*, to name a few.

Mary Mulari, United States

Mary Mulari's home is Aurora, Minnesota, where the cool, northern climate motivated her to create her first sweatshirt embellishments. An author and teacher, Mary has written 11 creative sewing books and developed an international reputation for her unique yet easy-to-sew clothing embellishments and her fun-filled seminars. She has appeared as a guest on "America Sews with Sue Hausmann" seen on PBS television. Her ideas appeal to sewing enthusiasts of all ability levels.

Lill Nylen, Sweden

Lill is the Director of Husqvarna Viking Academy, as well as Manager of Marketing Communication, at Viking Sewing Machines in Sweden. In that respect, she is responsible for the education of Husqvarna Viking dealers worldwide, and also for the production of Communication Material.

Lill is a graduate of Lennings Fashion Design College in Sweden and she also has a degree from the most prestigious school of Design and Pattern Construction in Sweden, "Tillskarar Akademin" in Stockholm. Upon her graduation, she was contacted by Husqvarna Viking and started to work for the sewing machine company immediately. She is the designer of many of the stitches, particularly the decorative stitches found on the Husqvarna Viking's sewing machines of today, as well as many of the embroidery designs.

She is also the author of several sewing books published in Scandinavia.

Martha Campbell Pullen, Ph.D., United States

Martha Campbell Pullen is an internationally known lecturer and teacher in the heirloom sewing field. Having learned to smock and French sew by machine more than 20 years ago, today Martha fronts her own heirloom sewing empire grown out of a small heirloom shop in Huntsville, Alabama. This successful venture boasts an importing lace and fabric business; the twice annual Martha Pullen Heirloom Sewing Schools; *SEW BEAUTIFUL* magazine; the PBS television series, "Martha's Sewing Room," and the consumer show, Martha's Sewing Market. As an author she has more than 25 books to her credit.

Michelle Pullen, Australia

Michelle's passion for sewing has seen her establish herself internationally as an embroidery designer. Specializing in machine cutwork, appliqué and Battenburg lace-making, she has self-published many related patterns and books on these subjects. Michelle is well known

ABOUT THE DESIGNERS

among Australian sewers from her many magazine editorials, sewing exhibitions, and educational weekends.

She is the founder of the Australia Sewing Guild, which was established with assistance from the American Guild.

Camille Remme, Canada

Canadian teacher and lecturer, Camille Remme is well-known among her fellow Canadian stitchers. As the author of several quilt books, *Frogs & Flowers, Braid & Chevron, Modular Magic, Birds & Bees, Starburst Mosaic,* and *Celtic Geometric Quilts,* Camille has also written for many magazines such as, *CANADA QUILTS, MINIATURE,* and Husqvarna Viking's *ZIGZAG.* She also contributed to *FIBERARTS, and Design Book Five.*

Inger Westerberg, Sweden

As an art teacher, freelance designer, and illustrator, Inger Westerberg has enjoyed a life of drawing, sewing, and knitting. She and her twin sister began sewing as children in Stockholm by helping each other make dresses with fabric their mother had purchased for them. Inger still enjoys sewing more then 40 years later. Since retiring, she has been enjoying life, her family and grandchild, while designing embroidery patterns for international use on the state-of-art Husqvarna Viking sewing machines.

Kerstin Widell, Sweden

Kerstin works for Viking Sewing Machines AB in Huskvarna, Sweden, as a research and development sewing consultant developing new products, accessories, and embroidery cards, etc.

Starting to sew by hand at the age of five, by 10 years old, she was sewing her own clothes on her mother's old treadle sewing machine. To encourage their daughter's budding hobby, Kerstin's parents bought her a Husqvarna Class 21. The machine made her sewing easier and much more fun since it worked on electricity and had both overcasting and decorative stitches. From this beginning, Kerstin completed an education in sewing and is a member in the Nordic quilt society.

Inetta Word, United States

A self-taught freelance sewing instructor from the United States, Inetta Word has taught numerous hands-on classes and written a variety of sewing books about and for Viking sewing machines. She has taught several workshops throughout the country for various sewing machine retailers on decorative work. Married and the proud mother and grandmother of two children respectively, Inetta is currently teaching classes on-line at the SewTech website.

Louise Baird, United States

Although Louise has been sewing for most of her life, she first became interested in machine art about 20 years ago when she took a class locally in free-motion embroidery, machine applique, and monogramming. Shortly thereafter, she attended a teacher training seminar for Speed Stitch, taught by Joyce Drexler. Approximately a year later, she met Martha Pullen and began teaching machine art classes in her new retail shop on Madison Street in Hunstville, AL. When Martha first began her Schools of Art Fashion, Louise was among one of the first teachers and has taught at most of the twice-yearly schools for the past 18 years.

After winning first place in the Machine Art contest sponsored by Sulky for three years running, she became a national Sulky educator about seven years ago and continues to teach for Sulky today. The co-author of *Elegant Concepts in Sulky* and the contributor to several other books in the Sulky Concepts series, she is also responsible for the applique directions in the book, *Applique: Martha's Favorites.* Louise has contributed to several other Martha Pullen publications, to Martha's magazine, *SEW BEAUTIFUL,* and appeared on the PBS series "Martha's Sewing Room" several times as well as sewing many of the projects and worked on the books that accompanied the series for the last six years. Louise wrote the section "OK...But I Don't Own an Embroidery Machine."

INDEX

INDEX

INDEX

METRIC EQUIVALENTS

Inches to Millimeters and Centimeters
MM - millimeters   CM - centimeters

Inches	MM	CM	Inches	CM	Inches	CM
1/8	3	0.3	9	22.9	30	76.2
1/4	6	0.6	10	25.4	31	78.7
3/8	10	1.0	11	27.9	32	81.3
1/2	13	1.3	12	30.5	33	83.8
5/8	16	1.6	13	33.0	34	86.4
3/4	19	1.9	14	35.6	35	88.9
7/8	22	2.2	15	38.1	36	91.4
1	25	2.5	16	40.6	37	94.0
1 1/4	32	3.2	17	43.2	38	96.5
1 1/2	38	3.8	18	45.7	39	99.1
1 3/4	44	4.4	19	48.3	40	101.6
2	51	5.1	20	50.8	41	104.1
2 1/2	64	6.4	21	53.3	42	106.7
3	76	7.6	22	55.9	43	109.2
3 1/2	89	8.9	23	58.4	44	111.8
4	102	10.2	24	61.0	45	114.3
4 1/2	114	11.4	25	63.5	46	116.8
5	127	12.7	26	66.0	47	119.4
6	152	15.2	27	68.6	48	121.9
7	178	17.8	28	71.1	49	124.5
8	203	20.3	29	73.7	50	127.0

METRIC CONVERSION CHART

Yards	Inches	Meters	Yards	Inches	Meters
1/8	4.5	0.11	1 1/8	40.5	1.03
1/4	9	0.23	1 1/4	45	1.14
3/8	13.5	0.34	1 3/8	49.5	1.26
1/2	18	0.46	1 1/2	54	1.37
5/8	22.5	0.57	1 5/8	58.5	1.49
3/4	27	0.69	1 3/4	63	1.60
7/8	31.5	0.80	1 7/8	67.5	1.71
1	36	0.91	2	72	1.83